Are American Elections Fair?

Are American Elections Fair?

Other books in the At Issue series:

Alternatives to Prisons
Anorexia
Antidepressants
Anti-Semitism
Are Privacy Rights Being Violated?
Biological and Chemical Weapons
Child Labor and Sweatshops
Child Sexual Abuse
Cosmetic Surgery
Creationism Versus Evolution
Do Children Have Rights?
Does Advertising Promote Substance Abuse?
Does the Internet Benefit Society?
Does the Internet Increase the Risk of Crime?
Drug Testing
The Ethics of Abortion
The Future of the Internet
How Can Domestic Violence Be Prevented?
How Can the Poor Be Helped?
How Does Religion Influence Politics?
How Should One Cope with Death?
How Should Society Address the Needs of the Elderly?
How Should the United States Treat Prisoners in the War on
    Terror?
How Should the World Respond to Natural Disasters?
Hurricane Katrina
Indian Gaming
Is American Culture in Decline?
Is Islam a Religion of War or Peace?
Islam in America
Is Poverty a Serious Threat?
Is the Gap Between the Rich and Poor Growing?
Is the Mafia Still a Force in America?
Is the World Heading Toward an Energy Crisis?
Is Torture Ever Justified?
Legalizing Drugs
Managing America's Forests
Nuclear and Toxic Waste
Prescription Drugs
Protecting America's Borders
Rain Forests
Religion and Education
Responding to the AIDS Epidemic
The Right to Die
School Shootings
Steroids
Teen Sex
What Causes Addiction?
What Is the State of Human Rights?

At ✳ Issue

Are American Elections Fair?

Stuart A. Kallen, *Book Editor*

Bonnie Szumski, *Publisher*
Helen Cothran, *Managing Editor*

GREENHAVEN PRESS
An imprint of Thomson Gale, a part of The Thomson Corporation

THOMSON
™
GALE

Detroit • New York • San Francisco • San Diego • New Haven, Conn.
Waterville, Maine • London • Munich

For more information, contact
Greenhaven Press
27500 Drake Rd.
Farmington Hills, MI 48331-3535
Or you can visit our Internet site at http://www.gale.com

Greenhaven Press anthologies primarily consist of previously published material taken from a variety of sources, including periodicals, books, scholarly journals, newspapers, government documents, and position papers from private and public organizations. These original sources are often edited for length and to ensure their accessibility for a young adult audience. The anthology editors also change the original titles of these works in order to clearly present the main thesis of each viewpoint and to explicitly indicate the opinion presented in the viewpoint. These alterations are made in consideration of both the reading and comprehension levels of a young adult audience. Every effort is made to ensure that Greenhaven Press accurately reflects the original intent of the authors included in this anthology.

LIBRARY OF CONGRESS CATALOGING-IN-PUBLICATION DATA
Are American elections fair? / Stuart A. Kallen, book editor.
p. cm. — (At issue)
Includes bibliographical references and index.
ISBN 0-7377-3378-0 (lib. : alk. paper) — ISBN 0-7377-3379-9 (pbk. : alk. paper)
1. Elections—United States. 2. Voting—United States. 3. Politics, Practical—United States. 4. United States—Politics and government. I. Kallen, Stuart A., 1955– . II. At issue (San Diego, Calif.)
JK1976.A83 2006
324.973—dc22   2005052339

Printed in the United States of America

Contents

	Page
Introduction	9

1. Political Fundraising Has Corrupted the Electoral Process   13
   Mark Green

2. Restricting Campaign Donations Violates Free Speech Rights   22
   Sheldon Richman

3. The Electoral College Should Be Abolished   28
   Lewis H. Lapham

4. The Electoral College Should Not Be Abolished   36
   Michael M. Uhlmann

5. Electronic Voting Machines Pose a Threat to Electoral Fairness   41
   Bev Harris and David Allen

6. Fears About Electronic Voting Machines Are Greatly Exaggerated   51
   John Fund

7. Felons Who Have Served Their Time Should Be Allowed to Vote   59
   Elizabeth Hull

8. Felons Should Not Be Allowed to Vote   68
   Christopher M. Tozzo

9. Illegal Aliens Should Not Be Allowed to Vote   71
   Michelle Malkin

10. Noncitizens Should Be Allowed to Participate in Elections   74
    Joaquin Avila

Organizations to Contact	79
Bibliography	83
Index	87

Introduction

Until November 2000, the majority of Americans believed in the fairness of elections. While African Americans had to fight for voting rights in the 1950s and 1960s, in the following decades there were only scattered instances of vote recounts or contested results. These problems usually occurred at local levels and were quickly resolved. However, the widespread trust in voting procedures was shaken in the 2000 presidential election between Democrat Albert Gore and Republican George W. Bush. In the run-up to the election, the race was nearly a dead heat, and few pollsters, election observers, or media analysts were willing to predict a winner. On November 7, after 101 million Americans had cast their votes, the outcome remained unclear. At first, television networks predicted that Gore had won the state of Florida, giving him enough electoral votes to become the forty-third president. Around 4:15 A.M. on November 8, however, the networks retracted their projections and announced the race was too close to call because the vote in Florida was nearly a tie.

By November 10, an automatic machine recount of ballots showed that Bush had won the state by only 374 votes. With such a close margin, Gore requested, and received, a hand recount in four Florida counties. In the following days, a small army of lawyers, political consultants, and politicians from both parties flocked to Florida to contest the validity of every questionable vote, attempting to disqualify as many opposition votes as possible.

As the recount process dragged on, it became clear that there were many flaws in the way that the election was conducted and with the methods used to count the ballots. Until the 2000 election, few citizens realized that ballots, voting machines, and ballot counting methods vary from state to state and even from county to county. For example, in Florida about 40 percent of the voters selected their candidates on optical scan ballots, using a pen or pencil to fill in an oval or connect dots on a paper ballot. A machine scans these ballots to count the votes and rejects ballots that are improperly marked (voters are immediately informed of the rejected ballot and allowed to revote). However, some voters in Palm Beach, many of them elderly Democrats, voted on "butterfly ballots" requiring voters to punch holes next to a candidate's name. Because of the confusing way the names were aligned on the ballots, some voters realized they had made a mistake and decided to change their votes midway through the process. This left hanging chads, small perforated pieces of paper that did not detach from the ballot. Other ballots were partially punched, leaving "pregnant chads." These ballots were rejected by automated counting machines, forcing elections officials to count them by hand or discard them as "spoilage." Eventually, out of nearly 6 million votes cast in Florida, approximately 179,855 ballots were regarded as spoilage for one reason or another and they were not counted in the official tally.

There were also problems with thousands of absentee ballots that were mailed in, mostly by those in the military, who tend to vote Republican. These ballots did not bear the necessary postmark to make them technically valid; items mailed from overseas military bases and navy ships often do not carry a cancellation date. While these types of ballots had been counted in previous elections, in this tight race lawyers for the Democrats decided to challenge the validity of the ballots. This decision sparked widespread outrage. A typical response was expressed in an e-mail written by Senior Chief Petty Officer Michael Gentry:

> This election, of all elections, may very well come down to that one vote that makes the difference. I and so many others like me who serve this great nation deserve to be heard! . . . We expect our leaders to serve us with the same honor, courage and commitment that we serve them. . . . The office of president affects those of us in the military more directly than any other citizen and counting our vote is simply the RIGHT THING TO DO!

December 12 was the deadline for the states to submit their roster of electoral voters, indicating which candidate had won each state's electoral votes. (According to the indirect system of voting in the United States, the candidate who wins the popular vote in a state receives all of the state's electoral votes.) As the December 12 deadline approached, the Republican-dominated Florida state legislature tried to pass a law to stop the recount, which would have given Florida's electoral votes to Bush. Gore, in turn, challenged this decision in the Florida Supreme Court. The Court allowed the count to continue, but Bush challenged the constitutionality of that decision.

After several other court challenges, the case *Bush v. Gore* eventually reached the U.S. Supreme Court. The Court concluded that Florida's method for recounting the votes was unreliable and could not be fixed before the December 12 deadline. Since the state could not guarantee that every vote would be accurately counted, the Court ruled that the recount denied Florida citizens the right to equal treatment under the law as guaranteed by the Fourteenth Amendment to the U.S. Constitution. The ruling stopped the recount thirty-seven days after the election. Ahead by 537 votes, Bush became president.

Republicans supported the Supreme Court's ruling, of course. As Richard A. Baehr writes on The American Thinker Web site: "The U.S. Supreme Court action probably prevented the theft of the election in Florida from occurring." Democrats disagreed, however, believing that the Republican majority of the Supreme Court did not base their decision on law but on their own political beliefs. As Yale law professor Akhil Reed Amar wrote,

> Many of us thought that the courts do not act in an openly political fashion. So this decision comes as a startling event that has shaken constitutional faith. It is not that scholars cared so much about the outcome, but the way it was done.

Many Democrats argued that it was unfair for Gore to lose the national election when he had won more than half a million votes more than Bush. The 2000 election was only the fourth time in history that the presidential candidate who did not receive a plurality of the popular vote won the majority of the electoral college vote.

The results of the 2000 election exposed many weak points in the American electoral system and had long-term consequences. Before the contested election, a Gallup poll showed that a full 97 percent of Americans believed that elections were fair. However, a 2004 Rasmussen Research poll revealed that figure had dropped to 57 percent. Experts worry that if citizens lose faith in the system, they will stop voting.

In a nation as politically divided as the United States, ballots are only one of the controversial aspects of elections.

Americans are also debating the accuracy of electronic voting machines, the influence of media polls, and the right of illegal immigrants to vote. With about half of the population voting for Republicans and the other half supporting Democrats, the debates over election fairness will continue well into the foreseeable future.

1

Political Fundraising Has Corrupted the Electoral Process

Mark Green

Mark Green was a candidate for mayor of New York City in 2001 and later founded the New Democracy Project, a public policy institute researching urban and national issues. He has been writing about campaign finance since 1972.

The political system has been taken over by an elite group of wealthy individuals who have the power to raise and spend tens of millions of dollars to get elected. With the ability to collect nearly ten times more money than their competitors, incumbents have a distinct advantage. Average Americans have little hope of participating or competing in such an unfair system. Unless a way is found to counter the influence of money on elections, fewer and fewer citizens will believe that American-style democracy represents the popular will of the people and the already low voter turnout rates will continue to fall.

As special-interest dollars in elections go up by the millions, voter participation goes down. While Israel reliably achieves over 80 percent turnout in its elections for prime minister, and France and the United Kingdom typically turn out about three quarters of their voting-age populations, the United States has not broken *60* percent since 1968. The turnout for American elections is no higher today than it was in the 1930s—with roughly half of eligible voters staying home in presidential elections, and nearly two thirds in congressional elections.

The 1988 presidential race between George H. Bush and Michael Dukakis had the worst turnout (50.1 percent) in 64 years, but that dubious honor was not held long: two cycles later, 1996's Clinton-Dole contest yielded a limp 49.1 percent. And four years after that, not even the tightness of 2000's Bush-Gore fight could inspire many more than half of registered voters to turn out. On the local level, the trends are similar. In a May 2002 Nebraska primary, a microscopic 20 percent of registered voters went to the polls, shattering the previous low mark of 36 percent.

> *The nation that prides itself on being the best example of government of, for, and by the people . . . is rapidly becoming a nation whose participation is limited to the interested or zealous few.*

When right-wing extremist Jean-Marie Le Pen took second place in France's 2002 presidential race, legions of press attributed the accused racist's surprise finish to the large number of so-called absent voters. Soberingly, the 72 percent turnout for that race—France's lowest in nearly four decades—is higher than any U.S. turnout in the twentieth century. "The nation that prides itself on being the best example of government of, for, and by the people," notes Curtis Gans, director of the nonpartisan Committee for the Study of the American Electorate, "is rapidly becoming a nation whose participation is limited to the interested or zealous few.". . .

More Money, Less Voter Participation

While from 1992 to 2000 soft money contributions increased five-fold, hard money nearly doubled, and party fund-raising tripled, voting in federal elections went *down* four percentage points overall. Obviously nothing can be done to change the statistical fact that one person's vote is highly unlikely to sway an election (although the tightness of [the] Bush-Gore [presidential race in 2000] should make voters think twice). But with the combination of incumbency and money apparently predetermining election results, many voters rationally assume their vote can't really matter.

This problem is of concern not just to liberals but to all small-*d* democrats. "We're perilously close to not having democracy," said Paul Weyrich, a prominent conservative who heads the Free Congress Foundation. "Non-voters are voting against the system, and if we get a bit more than that, the system won't work."

In an age when incumbency and money are mutually reinforcing and "redistricting" is little more than a synonym for "incumbent protecting," the realistic number of potentially competitive seats in general elections can be counted on one's fingers and toes. In fact, getting reelected has become so automatic that a member of Congress is almost more likely to vacate his or her seat by *dying* than by losing.

In both 1998 and 2000, more than 98 percent of House incumbents who sought reelection won their races. (Senate challengers fared slightly better, winning 10 percent and 18 percent, respectively.) In 1996, every single one of the 113 Congress members first elected in the 1980s won his or her race for reelection. All but 4 won by 10 percent or more, and 75 won by a whopping 30 percent or more. While 142 incumbents were defeated in the 1960s, that number fell to just 97 in the 1970s, to 88 in the 1980s, and to 102 in the 1990s. . . .

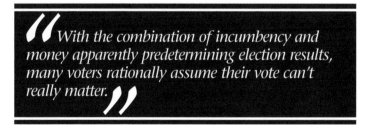

With the combination of incumbency and money apparently predetermining election results, many voters rationally assume their vote can't really matter.

In the context of fund-raising, the incumbent's advantage is largely predicated on money. Of course, the fact that incumbents can gerrymander districts once a decade also helps their bids for reelection but is marginal when compared with the potent mixture of money and incumbency. In 1988, incumbents ended up with twice as much in *leftover* funds as their challengers *spent*. In 2000, House incumbents outspent their challengers by better than 4 to 1 ($408.5 million to $89 million), enjoyed an 8-to-1 edge in PAC [political action committee] money, and by the end of October had a 13-to-1 advantage in cash on hand. Senate incumbents in 2000 raised $155.9 million, compared with $63 million by their challengers, and held a 6-to-1 edge in both PAC funds and cash on hand. [In 2004 Senate incumbents raised more than $223 million and maintained a similar advantage over challengers.]

With both Speaker Dennis Hastert [R-IL] and Representative Martin Frost (D-TX) bemoaning how terrible [the] McCain-Feingold [campaign finance reform bill] will be for their respective parties, one can't help but conclude that the two distinct political parties in Washington have given way to one monolithic alternative: the incumbent party.

> **"***Party leaders acknowledge that they explicitly try to recruit self-financing candidates, not necessarily the best candidates, to run.***"**

Carrying over war chests is one of the great time-honored traditions of the incumbency protection program. Amass as much cash as you possibly can—even if you have no known opponent—and then use it to intimidate potential challengers, who will drop out or never even run to begin with. Once re-election is achieved, the member of Congress carries over the war chest into the next campaign and the next and the next. In a very real sense rolling over such treasuries violates the spirit of the campaign finance contribution limits, since a John Donor may give Challenger X only $2000 for a particular campaign in a particular year but may have given Congressman Z a total of $8000 for a campaign against Challenger X ($2000 in each of four election cycles).

In Public Citizen's Congress Watch study *House Insurance: How the Permanent Congress Hoards Campaign Cash*, members of the 101st Congress were found to have over $67 million stowed away in campaign war chests *the month they took office*, "virtually assur[ing] reelection [and] certainly discourag[ing] qualified candidates from challenging the financially stronger representatives." According to the same Congress Watch report, 89 percent of House incumbents faced financially noncompetitive races in 2000, meaning they faced either no opposition or challengers with less than half their campaign resources.

The only ways to crack open this continuing "unfair advantage" are serious campaign finance reform or congressional term limits. And we'll get reform only when members of Congress start fearing limits on their terms more than they fear limits on their money.

The Money Chase

On any given workday, you can see streams of Congress members leaving their Capitol Hill offices to go to small campaign cubicles in order to dial for dollars. "The problem is much worse than portrayed," says Senator Ron Wyden (D-OR). "The money chase is so time-consuming that people should wonder how we have time to get anything done. Yes, the day after an election, people sleep in on Wednesday. But then the money chase starts in again, day after day, year in and year out.

"In an election year," he continued, "members have cards or Blackberrys that say '8–9 Grange; 9–10 Hearing on Technology; 10-4 money calls at DCCC.' For that much of the day, a significant number of public officials are sitting in a dank office away from their public office with their tin cup out instead of thinking about how to help their constituents."

Ask anyone involved in the game, and, if they're honest, the refrain will be the same. In his autobiography, [former New Jersey senator] Bill Bradley wrote that, despite his fame and popularity, he had to spend 40 percent of his freshman Senate term fund-raising for reelection. One New York congressman, well known for raising tons of special-interest money, confided at a fund-raiser in early 2002, "I spend almost half my time raising money." When asked if his job performance would change if he didn't have to fund-raise incessantly, the representative didn't hesitate. "Oh yes, I'd be much more independent and effective."

Even Senator Dick Durbin (D-IL), among the hardest working of senators, is candid enough to admit in an interview, "Of course I won't miss votes, but after that, fund-raising has to take precedence. We'll schedule fund-raisers and then build around them." Representative Sherrod Brown (D-OH) confides that he has three full-time jobs: "Congressman, campaigner, fund-raiser."

Senator Robert C. Byrd [of West Virginia] the longest-serving member of either chamber, put it best, calling his colleagues "part-time legislators and full-time fund-raisers." Senator Byrd told [reporter] Mark Shields that during his tenure as

Senate majority leader he often had to delay votes because of fund-raising conflicts. He mocked the parade of requests he endured for years: "Please, no votes Monday . . . no votes after four on Thursday . . . I've got a fund-raiser scheduled in Los Angeles . . . in New York . . . in my home state . . . "

Stanley Sheinbaum, a prominent Democratic donor and activist in California, grew so frustrated with members of Congress calling to ask for money that he told a high-ranking senator he would accept his request for a meeting only "on the proviso that money not be discussed." But given the rules of engagement, is it really a surprise that incumbents regard donors more as ATMs than as people, and that donors come to resent it?

The Money Chase Deters Talent from Seeking Office

Challengers know they must make it through a "money primary" first if they ever want to reach the "voters' primary"— and the polling place of donors can turn away anyone without secure financing, which of course deters potential contenders who have more talent than funds. "At some point," argues Joshua Rosenkranz of the Brennan Center for Justice, "the spending of money is less an exercise in speech, and more an exercise in raw power—the power to dominate the conversation and to scare away all potential challengers." Of course it's impossible to calculate how many good women and men decide not to seek office because of the prohibitive costs, but most astute observers assume that it's many. . . .

When Elizabeth Dole aborted her run for president in October 1999, money was the single reason she cited. She pointed to the 80-to-1 fund-raising edge George W. Bush held over her. "I hoped to compensate by attracting new people to the political process, by emphasizing experience and advocating substantive issues," she told a roomful of tearful supporters. "But as important as these things may be, the bottom line remains money."

Perhaps most alarming is the case of Reubin Askew. So vast and disquieting were the demands for money in Askew's 1988 Florida Senate race that the former governor abruptly dropped out—despite opinion polls showing him with a 4-to-1 lead in the primary and a 2-to-1 advantage in the general election. "Something is seriously wrong with our system," Askew explained, "when many candidates for the Senate need to spend

75 percent of their time raising money." As Askew's issues director for the campaign, Dexter Filkins, wrote, "The need to raise so much cash so fast limited Askew's contact with the average voter—that is, one who did not donate money. We simply didn't have time for them." If Askew, a popular elected official, couldn't handle the incessant demands of fund-raising, how do you suppose an unwealthy, unfamous, and unsubsidized workingman or -woman might make out?

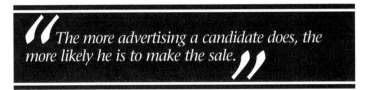

The more advertising a candidate does, the more likely he is to make the sale.

Of course, there's no formal "money primary" in the law or Constitution. All potential candidates are allowed to raise up to $1000 a donor per election or give themselves as much of their personal wealth as they can. "The law, in its majesty equality, permits the rich as well as the poor to sleep under bridges, to beg in the streets and steal bread," wrote [French writer] Anatole France, which inspired this extrapolation from the late U.S. Appellate Court Judge J. Skelly Wright: "The law, in its majestic equality, allows the poor as well as the rich to form political action committees, to purchase the most sophisticated polling, media and direct mail techniques and to drown out each other's voices by overwhelming expenditures in political campaigns. Financial inequities . . . undermine the political proposition to which this nation is dedicated—that all men are created equal."

These financial disparities account in part for why there are so few blue-collar workers in Congress. "Do you honestly think that a butcher could get elected to the Senate today?" Senator Byrd rhetorically asked. "A garbage collector? A small grocery man? A welder?"

The Money Chase Favors Multimillionaires

When soliciting funds from individuals and PACs turns out to be inadequate to cover the costs of campaigning, candidates will often supply the requisite funds by drawing from their personal finances. In 2000, twenty-seven House and Senate candidates spent at least $500,000 of their own money on their own campaigns. Self-financing is especially pronounced for challengers and for candidates in open-seat races. Challengers in the 1996 House elections spent an average of over $40,000 of their own money, one sixth of their total campaign costs; candidates in open-seat races spent over $90,000. The average Senate challenger that year spent $645,000—one quarter of his/her total campaign costs—out of his/her own pocket.

Already, more than a third of Senate members are millionaires—and the number keeps growing. At least 50 members of the two houses are multimillionaires, among them the following senators: John Kerry, with a net worth of $675 million; Jon Corzine, $400 million; Herbert Kohl (D-WI), $300 million; Jay Rockefeller IV (D-WV), $200 million; Peter Fitzgerald (R-IL), $50 million; Mark Dayton (D-MN), $20 million; and Bill Frist (R-TN), $20 million.

Asked why so many of the deep-pocketed senators are, surprisingly, Democrats, Senator Carl Levin laughs. "It's a growing solution to Republican money. Since we can't raise as much special-interest money, we look more for candidates who can spend their own." Corzine, a former Goldman Sachs CEO, agrees. "Democratic leaders more eagerly recruited [wealthy self-financers] to relieve financial pressure on the party and because more such Democrats [than Republicans] run believing that government does good things," New Jersey's junior senator explains. "There's a tradition from FDR to JFK of Democrats who do it to fix the world and level the playing field of society."

Indeed, party leaders acknowledge that they explicitly try to recruit self-financing candidates, not necessarily the best candidates, to run. But since [the Supreme Court ruling] *Buckley v. Valeo* permits the wealthy to contribute as much to their own campaigns as they like—because the Court reasoned a person can't corrupt *himself*, never considering how such spending could corrupt the *process*—the strategy is legal, and often a winning one. Think about the thousands of hours of fundraising that can be used for other things, like wooing party officials and opinion leaders, reaching out to voters, studying up on issues, and making news. Or the bottomless budget for television advertising that enables the candidate to flood the airwaves with her message.

Those who counter that advertisements don't force voters to vote for their candidates are correct, at least in a narrow sense. There's probably no amount of money that could persuade a majority to vote for [conservative commentator and former presidential candidate] Pat Buchanan. . . . But advertising is a $600-billion-a-year industry for a reason—and the reason is that, overall, the more advertising a candidate does, the more likely he is to make the sale. Or to raise doubts about an opponent who can't afford to rebut. . . .

Mark Schmitt of the Open Society Institute wrote, "The self-financed Democrats of most recent vintage . . . have all shown themselves to be as capable, liberal, and brave as their older counterparts like Jay Rockefeller. But there is no getting around the fact that the advantage of self-financed candidates has created a political plutocracy that looks less like America, economically, than at any time since before the direct election of senators."

If something doesn't change soon, there will be only three types of people running for and holding office in the future: super-fund-raisers, celebrities, and multimillionaires.

2

Restricting Campaign Donations Violates Free Speech Rights

Sheldon Richman

Sheldon Richman is a senior fellow at the Future of Freedom Foundation (FFF), a conservative think tank. He is also editor of the Foundation for Economic Education's magazine the Freeman *and author of* Tethered Citizens: Time to Repeal the Welfare State.

In an effort to regulate some of the billions of dollars that pour into political campaigns, Congress passed the McCain-Feingold Act in 2002, preventing political parties from using the "soft money" donated to their party's general fund for the election of federal candidates. While passed with good intent, McCain-Feingold has acted to restrict private citizens who wish to raise money for political ads for specific candidates. By curtailing fund-raising activities, Congress is attempting to limit the right to free speech guaranteed in the Constitution. The McCain-Feingold Act limits electoral participation by those who wish to make their voices heard through political donations and allows politicians to censor criticism of themselves in the media.

It didn't take long for the sponsors of the latest campaign-finance reform (translation: free-speech prohibitions) to complain that their law is being circumvented. Senators John McCain (Republicrat) and Russell Feingold (Demoblican) are infuriated that private groups are using (gasp!) unregulated money to influence an election and their law doesn't seem to be able to stop it.

The McCain-Feingold law, also known as the Bipartisan Campaign Reform Act, forbids political parties from raising unrestricted "soft money" and using it to elect federal candidates. Predictably, people quickly found ways to accomplish their ends without using the parties' fund-raising machinery. The law already permitted (how merciful) what are called "527 committees," named after a section of the tax code. These are private groups that raise money from unions, corporations, and individuals for the purpose of influencing elections. They can raise all the money they want and spend what they raise as long as they don't coordinate with the campaign organizations.

This naturally upsets some folks, such as politicians who abhor the idea that private citizens might run television ads that attack incumbents like themselves.

Most of the "527" activity is coming from opponents of President George W. Bush. The Media Fund and other Democrat-leaning groups are accused of being a "shadow party," because they're doing what the Democratic National Committee would be doing if Congress and Bush hadn't enacted the law. McCain and Feingold want the Federal Election Commission (FEC) to impose regulations to stop that activity. The Bush-Cheney campaign has also complained to the FEC about these groups' alleged circumvention of the law.

Some Republican sympathizers worry about the coming crackdown, but the Republican establishment seems unconcerned. This has a simple explanation: Republicans raise far more "hard money" (restricted money given directly to candidates) than the Democrats do and so don't care as much about soft money.

A Misuse of Government Power

Let's be clear about what's happening here. The Republican-controlled Congress passed flagrant prohibitions on fund-raising and free speech by political parties and their supporters. A Republican president signed the bill. The U.S. Supreme Court affirmed its constitutionality. As a result, nonparty organizations run by former Democratic operatives are raising money and airing commercials critical of the president. So the president and other Republicans (and some Democrats) want the FEC to stop those organizations in their tracks.

All this is happening in a putatively free country. . . .

McCain-Feingold had nothing to do with fears that money would corrupt politics. No member of Congress was willing to say, "We need a prohibition on soft money and tight controls on hard money because I am weak and prone to what is in effect bribery, that is, voting as my rich donors wish." No one said that, although they left the public with the impression that corruption was their chief concern.

> ❝ *The Republican-controlled Congress passed flagrant prohibitions on fund-raising and free speech by political parties and their supporters.* ❞

In reality, they wanted "reform" because they think campaigns are too negative and too expensive. In other words, they dislike that incumbents can be criticized during campaigns by people who raise money and air television commercials. They didn't emphasize that concern because it is blatantly self-serving. Is it any of their business how much money the American people choose to spend on campaigns? Is prohibiting campaign negativism a proper use of government power?

Money and Politics

The issue of money in politics is ironic. Politics attracts money because government is powerful. There is a simple way to make corporate executives and other "special interests" indifferent to political campaigns: strip the politicians of their power to favor or hamper private interests. Short of that, nothing will succeed in keeping money out of politics. If "527" activity is outlawed, other ways will be found. It's a sure thing.

The allegations about corruption get more interesting the closer they are examined. Is it corruption if a company donates to a like-minded candidate, who then votes the way the company prefers? After all, the company wouldn't have contributed to a hostile candidate. To demand that companies, unions, and advocacy organizations be barred from participating in campaigns is to betray a lack of confidence in democracy. There's nothing wrong with lacking confidence, but the finance reformers should at least have the decency to say so. Instead, they attack the freedom to participate in elections while praising democracy. It's a contradiction.

Another thing that gets more interesting under the microscope is the idea that corporations relish pouring millions of dollars into political coffers and shriek at such laws as McCain-Feingold. It ain't necessarily so.

Corporations Favor Reform Bill

It is certainly true that throughout American history some business interests sought extra-market favors from politicians. But here's a riddle: If corporations are so powerful that we need McCain-Feingold, how did it ever pass?

[Law professor] Robert H. Sitkoff, writing in the Winter 2003–2004 issue of the Cato Institute's *Regulation* magazine, has an answer. Maybe the powerful corporate interests weren't opposed to the bill at all. But if that's true, why weren't they?

To answer this question, Sitkoff goes back to 1907, when the first campaign-finance reform, the Tillman Act, was passed. It outlawed corporate donations to federal candidates. The naive story of this law is that progressive-minded people, such as President Theodore Roosevelt, overcame great odds to tame political abuses by robber barons. It wasn't quite that way.

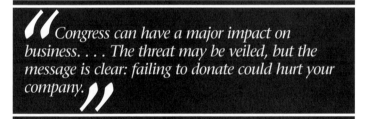

Congress can have a major impact on business. . . . The threat may be veiled, but the message is clear: failing to donate could hurt your company.

While there was some public anxiety about corporate influence in politics, the nature of the influence is critical. Sitkoff points out that in the late 19th century, "the national parties began shouldering a larger share of the [financial] burden" in elections. Hence, "the national parties began deploying systematic procedures for *demanding contributions* for their candidates—and corporations were a frequent target." [Emphasis added.]

Sitkoff notes that in 1896, when Republican William McKinley faced Democrat William Jennings Bryan for the presidency, monetary policy was the chief issue. McKinley's money man, Mark Hanna, "focused his efforts on New York financiers and large corporations. Standard Oil was *assessed* $250,000 and, under Hanna's stewardship, the Republican National Committee *assessed* banks at one-quarter of one percent of their capital." [Emphasis added.] Hanna's letters "requesting" donations would mention what a company's competitors had already given.

Blackmail and Extortion

Thus the background to "campaign finance reform" was an environment in which powerful politicians had their henchmen lean on businesses in order to raise money. In 1907, Sitkoff notes, the *New York Times* recognized what was happening. In an editorial the *Times* anticipated that the Tillman Act "will lessen a very mean and sordid practice of *blackmail*. The beneficiaries [of regulation] will still find methods of furnishing the sinews of war to the party that controls their favors, but the great number of corporations that have *suffered extortion* through weakness and cowardice will have their backbones stiffened, and parties will be put to it to fill their coffers by *really voluntary* contributions." [Emphasis added.]

As Sitkoff writes,

> This is not to say that, in the late 1800s and early 1900s, corporations were not engaged in socially undesirable rent seeking. Rather, the point is that legislators are as active in the "market for legislation" as potential "buyers" such as corporations.

This is true today. Politicians make it perfectly obvious that donations can bring benefits. Even worse, they make it clear that donations can ward off detrimental legislation. . . .

Summing up, Sitkoff writes,

> To the extent that legislators actively raise funds through threats and other means, [business's] acquiescing in a ban on direct corporation contributions would be a rational response. Not surprisingly, corporate leaders embraced the Tillman Act for precisely that reason.

"Not Easy Saying No"

In other words, business welcomed relief from the political squeeze for money. Why? Corporate managers thought they had better things to do with their companies' money than to hand it over to politicians—such as improve their products or develop new ones. Economic, as opposed to political, investment was likely to increase the stock price and keep the shareholders (their bosses) happy. But failing to cough up political money on demand, especially when one's competitors are doing it, could be bad for the company's health. So a manager might conclude he had no choice but to give—unless corporate donations could be *outlawed.*

That was why businessmen supported the earliest campaign finance act, and that is why corporate opposition to McCain-Feingold was conspicuous by its absence. Sitkoff quotes a corporate manager who said in connection with McCain-Feingold, most "business today would prefer not to give. But there's not going to be unilateral disarmament." He also quotes the global chairman of Deloitte Touche Tomatsu at the time:

> What has been called legislated bribery looks like extortion to us. . . . I know from personal experience and from other executives that it's not easy saying no to appeals for cash from powerful members of Congress or their operatives. Congress can have a major impact on business. . . . The threat may be veiled, but the message is clear: failing to donate could hurt your company.

McCain-Feingold may actually give some desired relief to beleaguered corporations. But, alas, it will do so by violating the free-speech rights of the American people. A better way would be to separate state and economy. How many businesses are willing to stand up for that?

3

The Electoral College Should Be Abolished

Lewis H. Lapham

Lewis H. Lapham is the editor of Harper's Magazine.

When the Founding Fathers wrote the Constitution, they created the Electoral College, a body of electors from each state who cast votes for the president. Under this system, the candidate who receives the majority of the direct popular vote in a state receives all the electoral votes for that state. This system of electing a chief executive is undemocratic because the final outcome may not reflect the will of the majority of Americans. As recently as the 2000 presidential elections, George W. Bush received a smaller number of popular votes than the opposing candidate Al Gore, but was elected president because he was awarded a greater number of electoral votes. The Electoral College, originally designed to give smaller states a voice in elections, has become an anachronism in the twenty-first century and has undercut voter confidence in the electoral process. Congress should therefore enact a Constitutional amendment to dissolve the Electoral College and allow the president to be elected by direct popular vote. Unless the chief executive is chosen by popular vote, millions of citizens will dispute the president's legitimacy and power.

If I lived in Cleveland or Detroit, my vote in the November presidential election might count for something in the eventual result; because I live in New York, it will count for nothing, as pointless as would be my vote for the next president of

Lewis H. Lapham, "Straw Votes," *Harper's Magazine*, vol. 309, November 2004, p. 7.

Uzbekistan or France. Roughly two thirds of the American electorate is similarly disenfranchised, and so it comes as no surprise that the autumn [2004] campaign season has brought with it a dense fog of slander in all categories of informed and uninformed opinion (Democrat and Republican, military and civilian, urban as well as rural and suburban) spewed forth by diminished citizens in both the red states and the blue[1] who apparently take comfort in their feelings of resentment, alienation, and rage.

The American people don't choose the American president; the decision rests with the Electoral College, which, as was made plain [in 2000] . . . in Florida may or may not reflect the popular will. The variance is deliberate, intended by the framers of the Constitution as a defense against the corruption of a federal legislature too easily bought and sold and as a check on the ignorant passions of an unlettered populace widely dispersed in what was still a wilderness. The Electoral College in the late eighteenth century recruited its members from among the most enlightened citizens in each of the states, men "free from any sinister bias," as well read as they were well traveled, admired for their "virtue," "discernment," and "information." By 1828 the theory of appointing wise counselors had given way to the practice of employing partisan stooges, but the Electoral College continues to exclude ordinary, run-of-the-mill Americans from the privilege of direct participation in the naming of the individual to whom they entrust the administration of their government. Which is why, together with everybody else in the country on Election Day, I won't vote for Senator John Kerry or President George W. Bush; I'll vote instead for thirty-one unknown persons [in the Electoral College] pledged to a line on the ballot and chosen for no reason other than their reliably sinister bias.

An Anti-Democratic Procedure

The Constitution assigns to each state a specific number of electors, the size of the delegation based on population and representation in Congress—fifty-five for California, twenty-one for Illinois, three for Wyoming, etc. Acting as freight-

---

1. "Red states" are those states in which the majority of people vote for the Republican candidate, while the "blue states" are those that vote for the Democratic candidate.

forwarding agents for the plurality of votes cast in each state, the electors come together in fifty state capitols on the first Monday after the second Wednesday in December, and there, in the presence of flags and usually at noon, they transfer the entire allotment of their state's electoral vote to the candidate on the winning side of the percentage. They take no notice of, nor grant any standing to, the concerns, wishes, views, theories, or convictions on the losing side of the percentage. On November 7, 2000, nearly 3 million people in Florida voted for Vice President Al Gore, but because Governor George W. Bush received the plurality (by a disputed margin of 537 votes), the Electoral College awarded him every vote cast for Gore and thus one more than the requisite majority of 270 in the Electoral College. Although in voting booths across the whole of the country Gore received 539,893 more popular votes than Bush, the single electoral vote, buttressed by the Supreme Court's decision to forbid a final recount in Florida, placed Bush in the White House.

> *The American people don't choose the American president; the decision rests with the Electoral College, which . . . may or may not reflect the popular will.*

In a new book published [in 2004] under the title *Why the Electoral College Is Bad for America*, George C. Edwards III, a professor of political science at Texas A&M University, explains the anti-democratic procedure and result in December 2000 with reference to the Bible lesson given at Matthew 13:12: "For whosoever hath, to him shall be given, and he shall have more abundance: but whosoever hath not, from him shall be taken away even that he hath." The same words describe the method of the Bush Administration in both its foreign and domestic theaters of operation, and in our current state of political animosity and confusion, I've come across few books as timely or as relevant as the one in which Professor Edwards suggests that the country now finds itself confronted not only with an absence of a coherent national politics but also with a constitutional crisis.

Unable to see how a democracy can call itself a democracy

unless everybody's vote is counted as equal, Professor Edwards sets out to prove that the Electoral College is both needlessly complex and inherently unjust. He informs his treatise with statistical tabulations (of election returns, presidential travel schedules, placement of campaign advertisements), with historical points of comparison (the elections of 1876, 1888, and 1960 discussed as foreshadowings of the election of 2000), and with firm refutations of the several contemporary pleadings put forward on behalf of the Electoral College as a necessary support of the two-party system. Other scholars in other rooms undoubtedly will quarrel with one or another of the professor's conclusions, but his principal lines of argument deserve extensive debate in both the news media and the Congress.

Some Votes Are More Equal than Others

Seeking to balance the interests of the larger states with those of the smaller states, delegates to the Constitutional Convention in 1787 devised the "Great Compromise" that apportioned seats in the House of Representatives according to the size of the state's population but assigned to each state, no matter how sparsely settled, two seats in the Senate. The deal was falsely named—not a compromise but a concession to the smaller states threatening to withhold ratification of the Constitution unless they received an equal share of America's newly acquired political inheritance. Writing in *Harper's Magazine* last [2004] Richard Rosenfeld described the consequences:

> In America today, U.S. senators from the twenty-six smallest states, representing a mere 18 percent of the nation's population, hold a majority in the United States Senate, and, therefore, under the Constitution, regardless of what the President, the House of Representatives, or even an overwhelming majority of the American people wants, nothing becomes law if those senators object.

For the same reasons that dictated the undemocratic organization of the Senate, the Electoral College under-represents large states and over-represents small states. As Professor Edwards points out, an electoral vote in Wyoming presently corresponds to 167,081 persons; an electoral vote in California represents 645,172 persons; which means that in a presidential election a popular vote in Cheyenne is the equivalent of four popular votes in Los Angeles or San Luis Obispo. The democratic faith in majority rule sustains and validates every other form of American election, but the election of the president takes place in an alternate universe.

The Imaginary Majority

Voters unaligned with the state's electoral vote play no part in the presidential election, and their voices disappear from the national political stage. The majority of the country's African Americans live in the southern states, their presence unremarked upon and their concerns unaddressed by either presidential candidate, because the southern states routinely deliver their electoral vote to the Republicans. Similarly, in the New England states, the electoral vote routinely goes to the Democrats, with the result that both presidential campaigns ignore the presence of conservative, socialist, libertarian, or independently minded voters in Rhode island and Connecticut. Comparable to the demographic charts governing the sale and distribution of consumer products, the tally in the Electoral College presents a distorted picture of the American character and mind—too much emphasis assigned to the Christian fundamentalism in the South as well as to the secular humanism in the North, not enough recognition of the diversity of opinion in small towns as well as in large cities.

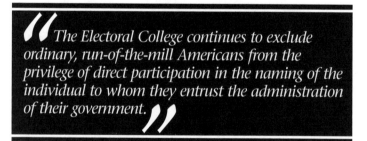

The Electoral College continues to exclude ordinary, run-of-the-mill Americans from the privilege of direct participation in the naming of the individual to whom they entrust the administration of their government.

Election by a majority of states rather than by a majority of citizens excuses the candidates from the effort of talking to, much less attempting to convince or persuade, voters not already inclined to applaud most everything they say or promise. . . . [In 2000] neither George Bush nor Al Gore spent much time campaigning in Texas, California, or New York, three states that among them encompassed 26 percent of the American population but possessed no electoral votes deemed to be negotiable—

the 32 in Texas on consignment to Bush, the 33 in New York and the 54 in California reserved to Gore. The two candidates in 2000 made a combined total of eighteen appearances in Wisconsin, thirty-one in Michigan, and twenty-six in Florida; neither of them appeared, not even once, in any of the eighteen states (among them Vermont, Oklahoma, Colorado, and Connecticut) regarded as dead letters and foregone conclusions.

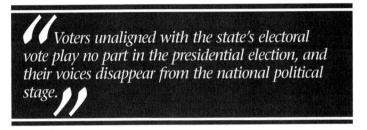

Voters unaligned with the state's electoral vote play no part in the presidential election, and their voices disappear from the national political stage.

The disproportionate investment of time and money in the so-called swing or battleground states is a measure of the degree to which the value of an American citizen has been discounted and debased. The presidential candidates don't address the American people simply as their fellow countrymen; they speak to an aggregate of interest groups and target audiences—Americans distinguished not by the fact of being American but by those of their ancillary characteristics that reduce them to a commodity: as a female American, a white American, a gay American, a black American, a Jewish American, a Native American, a swing-state American. The subordination of the noun to the adjective makes a mockery of the democratic premise, but it serves the marketing strategy of a campaign directed at the Electoral College, and it substitutes for a unified American or national interest an incoherent miscellany of state or special interests. Which is why the naming of the next president of the United States can turn not on a question important to the country as a whole but on a sentiment dear to the hearts of the Cuban Americans in the swing state of Florida. . . .

"The Vital Principle of Republican Government"

By doing away with the Electoral College we wouldn't cure all the ills that currently afflict the American democracy—the state of political paralysis that follows from the two-party system, unrepresentative government in the Senate, etc.—but at the very least we might make a beginning. The reform would strengthen what James Madison once called "the vital principle of republican government"—one man, one vote, the will of the majority, the belief that all of us have an equal say in the matter. We prove ourselves citizens of a democracy not by our winning of elections but by our agreeing to lose elections. The deal is hard to make, and the consent of the governed not freely given, unless we think ourselves participant in the election. If my vote doesn't count, I have no stake in the outcome, no reason to accept responsibility for, or acquire knowledge of, either the good or evil done in my name by the government in Washington. A CBS/*New York Times* poll taken in May 2003 (i.e., twenty months after the collapse of the World Trade Center and eight weeks after the invasion of Iraq) discovered 38 percent of the respondents refusing to regard George W. Bush as the legitimate president of the United States, a finding that accounts for a good deal of the rancor in [the 2004] election campaign.

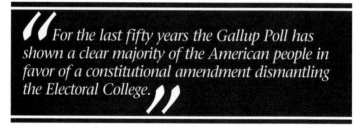

> For the last fifty years the Gallup Poll has shown a clear majority of the American people in favor of a constitutional amendment dismantling the Electoral College.

Since the inception of the republic, a central theme in the American political story has been the one about the further broadening of the electorate and thus the further democratization of the Constitution. The intention has been abetted and approved by politicians as distant from one another in time and place as Presidents James Madison and Andrew Jackson, Senators Estes Kefauver, Hubert Humphrey, and Margaret Chase Smith. Five of the seventeen amendments added to the Bill of Rights since 1791 have expanded the electorate—the Fifteenth in 1870 (extending the vote to former slaves), the Nineteenth in 1920 (presenting the vote to women), the Twenty-third in 1961 (granting the vote to residents of Washington, D.C.), the Twenty-fourth in 1964 (prohibiting poll taxes), and the Twenty-sixth in 1971 (welcoming voters to the polls at the age of eighteen). For the last fifty years the Gallup Poll has shown a clear majority of the American people in favor of a constitutional amendment dismantling the Electoral College; [in 2001] the poll reported "little question" on the part of the American public about going to "a direct popular vote for the presidency." In 1969 and again ten years later, the Congress nearly passed the necessary legislation, both attempts endorsed by strong majorities in the House but failing, narrowly, in the Senate.

Professor Edwards observes that for more than 200 years the country has survived the consequences of the variance between the popular and the electoral vote (the accession to the White House of Rutherford B. Hayes in 1876, of Benjamin Harrison in 1888), but I don't think that our luck is likely to hold for another three months, let alone another decade or century. In no prior election season can I remember talking to so many people who say, bitterly and seriously, that they intend to leave the country if their candidate fails to win the White House. Having lost faith in both the theory and practice of democratic self-government, they look upon the election in the manner of spectators at a bad play, amused or not amused by the whirl and spin of libel in the news media but believing themselves absent from the long and continuing American struggle (brave, dangerous, always against the odds) to secure a government of laws, not men.

Their indifference doesn't bode well for the country's future prospects, and maybe we should count ourselves fortunate if [future elections result] . . . in stalemate, suspicion, and dispute. The circumstance would oblige us to rediscover the purpose and meaning of democracy, to realign our political thought, and therefore the Constitution, with circumstances far different from those existing in the late eighteenth century, to elect as president a man or woman representing the whole of our national identity rather than the smiling face of a focus-group Caesar or Napoleon striking heroic military poses in a swing-state shopping mall.

4

The Electoral College Should Not Be Abolished

Michael M. Uhlmann

Michael M. Uhlmann teaches politics and policy at the Claremont Graduate University in California.

The Electoral College protects citizens in less populous states from the political whims of those in cities and densely populated areas. Under the electoral system, candidates must appeal to the varied interests of voters in smaller states in order to gather the largest number of electoral votes. When the framers of the Constitution designed the Electoral College, they understood that such a system was necessary to protect the desires of the minority from what the fourth president, James Madison, called the "tyranny of the majority." The Electoral College has served the nation well for more than two centuries. Switching to a system of direct popular voting would give unrestrained power to the majority and violate the rights of the minority.

As the late [comedian] Rodney Dangerfield might say, the Electoral College just don't get no respect. Polls show that most Americans, given the opportunity, would cashier it tomorrow in favor of so-called direct election. That they'd live to regret their decision only reminds us of [social critic] H.L. Mencken's definition of democracy: a form of government in which the people know what they want, and deserve to get it

Michael M. Uhlmann, "The Old (Electoral) College Cheer: Why We Have It; Why We Need It," *National Review*, vol. 56, November 8, 2004, p. 28. Copyright © 2004 by National Review, Inc., 215 Lexington Avenue, New York, NY 10016. Reproduced by permission.

good and hard. What the people would get by choosing direct election is the disintegration of the state-based two-party system; the rise of numerous factional parties based on region, class, ideology, or cult of personality; radicalized public opinion, frequent runoff elections, widespread electoral fraud, and centralized control of the electoral process; and, ultimately, unstable national government that veers between incompetence and tyrannical caprice. And that's only a partial list.

Dissatisfaction with the electoral-vote system has been a staple of populist rhetoric ever since presidential elections became fully democratized in the 1820s. More than 700 constitutional amendments have been introduced to change the system—by far the greatest number on any subject—and although reform prescriptions have varied greatly in detail, their common assumption has always been that our electoral rules prevent the true voice of the people from being heard.

But what is the "true voice" of the people? Public sentiment can be expressed and measured in any number of ways, but not all are conducive to securing rights. If ascertaining the consent of the people were only a matter of counting heads until you got to 50 percent plus one, we could dispense with most of the distinctive features of the Constitution—not only electoral votes, but also federalism, the separation of powers, bicameralism and staggered elections. All these devices depart from simple majoritarianism, and for good reason: Men do not suddenly become angels when they acquire the right to vote; an electoral majority can be just as tyrannical as autocratic kings or corrupt oligarchs.

> *The Constitution understands elections not as ends in themselves, but as a means of securing limited government and equal rights for all.*

The Founders believed that while the selfish proclivities of human nature could not be eliminated, their baleful effects could be mitigated by a properly designed constitutional structure. Although the Constitution recognizes no other source of authority than the people, it takes pains to shape and channel popular consent in very particular ways. Thomas Jefferson perfectly captured the Framers' intent in his First Inaugural Address: "All, too, will bear in mind this sacred principle, that though the will of the majority is in all cases to prevail, that will to be rightful must be reasonable; that the minority possess their equal rights, which equal law must protect, and to violate which would be oppression." By reasonable majorities, Jefferson meant those that would reflect popular sentiment but, by the very manner of their composition, would be unable or unlikely to suppress the rights and interests of those in the minority. Accordingly, the Constitution understands elections not as ends in themselves, but as a means of securing limited government and equal rights for all.

Supporting a Two-Party System

The presidential election system helps to form reasonable majorities through the interaction of its three distinguishing attributes: the distribution and apportionment of electoral votes in accordance with the federal principle; the requirement that the winner garner a majority of electoral votes; and the custom (followed by 48 of 50 states) of awarding all of a state's electoral votes to the popular-vote victor within that state. Working together, these features link the presidency to the federal system, discourage third parties, and induce moderation on the part of candidates and interest groups alike. No candidate can win without a broad national coalition, assembled state by state yet compelled to transcend narrow geographic, economic, and social interests.

Reformers tend to assume that the mode of the presidential election can be changed without affecting anything else. Not so. As Sen. John F. Kennedy argued in the 1950s, by changing the method of the presidential election, you change not only the presidency but the entire political solar system of which it is an integral part. The presidency is at once the apex of our constitutional structure and the grand prize of the party system. Our method of selecting a president is the linchpin that holds both together. Capturing the presidency is the principal raison d'etre of our political parties, whose structure, thanks to the electoral-vote system, mirrors the uniquely federal structure of the Constitution. This means that two-party competition is the norm; in a country of America's size and diversity, that is no small virtue.

With (for the most part) only two parties in contention, the major candidates are forced to appeal to most of the same voters. This drives them both toward the center, moderates their campaign rhetoric, and helps the winner to govern more effectively once in office. Many factional interests, for their part, are under a reciprocal inducement to buy insurance with both sides, meaning the compromises necessary for successful rule will be made prior to and not after the election. Moreover, by making the states the principal electoral battlegrounds, the current system tends to insulate the nation against the effects of local voting fraud. All in all, the current system forces the ambitions of presidential candidates into the same constitutional mold that defines and tempers American political life as a whole. It thereby prevents the presidency from becoming a potentially dangerous tutelary force separate and apart from the rest of the Constitution's structure.

A Radical Concept

These and other salutary consequences would disappear under direct election, whose deceptive simplicities mask its truly radical character. . . . We came perilously close to enacting direct election following the 1968 contest, when George Wallace's third-party candidacy shattered the New Deal coalition of big-city machines and the one-party South. Fearing the long-run effects of Republican competition in the New South, Democrats tried to change the rules to their advantage. They will do so again as soon as the opportunity seems propitious. . . .

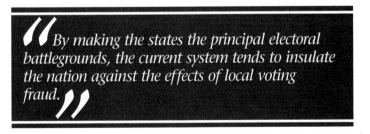

By making the states the principal electoral battlegrounds, the current system tends to insulate the nation against the effects of local voting fraud.

In 1969, as President [Richard M.] Nixon dithered and eventually ducked, direct election passed the House by a sizeable constitutional majority—including many Republicans who ought to have known better. But for a small and determined group of conservative Democratic and Republican senators who filibustered it to death, direct election would have been presented to the states in an atmosphere that greatly favored ratification. Sensible heads may prevail in today's [2004]

Republican-controlled House, but don't count on it: On matters of electoral reform especially, congressmen have little stomach for resisting populist enthusiasms. A House that rolled over for McCain-Feingold [a bill for campaign finance reform] which enjoyed only mild public support, will not likely oppose the clamor for direct election. As for today's Senate, one would be hard pressed to identify a band of constitutional stalwarts comparable to those who courageously resisted popular currents in 1970. The next few years, in short, may test whether our nation has the patience or wisdom to preserve the delicate balances of our constitutional solar system.

Proponents of direct election indict those delicate balances for being "undemocratic." That is true only in the most superficial sense. If the Electoral College is undemocratic, so are federalism, the United States Senate, and the procedure for constitutional amendment. So is bicameralism and, for that matter, the separation of powers, which among other things authorizes an unelected judiciary. These constitutional devices were once widely understood to be the very heart and soul of the effort to form reasonable majorities. If all you care about is the achievement of mathematical equality in presidential elections, and if to achieve that goal you're willing to eliminate the states' role in presidential elections, what other "undemocratic" features of the Constitution are you also willing to destroy? And when you're done hacking your way through the Constitution, what guarantee can you give that your mathematically equal majorities can be restrained? How will you constrain the ambitions of presidents who claim to be the only authentic voice of the people?

The current system teaches us that the character of a majority is more important than its size alone. Americans ought to care about whether the winner's support is spread across a broad geographic area and a wide spectrum of interests. That is what enables presidents to govern more effectively—and what encourages them to govern more justly than they would if their majority were gathered from, say, an aggregation of heavy population centers. By ensuring that the winner's majority reflects the diversity of our uniquely federated republic, the current system also assures his opposition that it will not have to fear for its life, liberty, or property. Direct election can provide no such assurance and may, in fact, guarantee just the opposite.

5

Electronic Voting Machines Pose a Threat to Electoral Fairness

Bev Harris and David Allen

Bev Harris is a freelance journalist who began writing about electronic voting machines in October 2002. She is credited with being among the first journalists to expose the problems with e-voting, and her research has been cited by the New York Times, Mother Jones, *CNN, CBS News, and Fox News. David Allen is a freelance writer, publisher, and computer systems engineer.*

Electronic voting machines have been put into service in hundreds of legislative districts across the country. Unfortunately these computerized machines are prone to glitches, crashes, and security breaches. In the past decade, there have been dozens of elections that have been unfairly decided because of problems with computer voting machines. The companies that make these machines downplay and dismiss charges of inaccuracy by critics and claim that their voting machines are amazingly accurate. Until the producers of electronic-voting machines confront the problems and are able to guarantee that every vote is fairly and accurately counted, those machines should be banned from further use.

In the Alabama 2002 general election, machines made by Election Systems and Software (ES&S) flipped the governor's race. Six thousand three hundred Baldwin County electronic votes

Bev Harris and David Allen, "Can We Trust These Machines?" *Black Box Voting: Ballot Tampering in the 21st Century,* edited by Lex Alexander. High Point, NC: Plan Nine Publications, 2003. Copyright © 2003 by Bev Harris. All rights reserved. Reproduced by permission.

mysteriously disappeared after polls had closed and everyone had gone home. Democrat Don Siegelman's victory was handed to Republican Bob Riley, and the recount Siegelman requested was denied. Six months after the election, the vendor still shrugged. "Something happened. I don't have enough intelligence to say exactly what," said Mark Kelley of ES&S.

When I began researching this story in October 2002, the media was reporting that electronic voting machines are fun and speedy, but I looked in vain for articles reporting that they are accurate. I discovered four magic words, "voting machines and glitch," which, when entered into the DJInteractive.com search engine, yielded a shocking result: A staggering pile of miscounts was accumulating. These were reported locally but had never been compiled in a single place, so reporters were missing a disturbing pattern.

Major Glitches and Miscounted Votes

I published a compendium of 56 documented cases in which voting machines had gotten it wrong.

How do voting machine makers respond to these reports? With shrugs. They indicate that their miscounts are nothing to be concerned about. One of their favorite phrases is: "It didn't change the result."

Except, of course, when it did:

In the 2002 general election, a computer miscount overturned the House District 11 result in Wayne County, North Carolina. Incorrect programming caused machines to skip over several thousand party-line votes, both Republican and Democratic. Fixing the error turned up 5,500 more votes and reversed the election for state representative.

This crushing defeat never happened. Voting machines failed to tally "yes" votes on the 2002 school bond issue in Gretna, Nebraska. This error gave the false impression that the measure had failed miserably, but it actually passed by a 2-to-1 margin. Responsibility for the errors was attributed to ES&S, the Omaha company that had provided the ballots and the machines.

According to the *Chicago Tribune*, "It was like being queen for a day—but only for 12 hours," said Richard Miholic, a losing Republican candidate for alderman who was told that he had won a Lake County, Illinois, primary election. He was among 15 people in four races affected by an ES&S vote-counting foul-up in the Chicago area.

An Orange County, California, election computer made a 100 per cent error during the April 1998 school bond referendum. The Registrar of Voters office initially announced that the bond issue had lost by a wide margin; in fact, it was supported by a majority of the ballots cast. The error was attributed to a programmer's reversing the "yes" and "no" answers in the software used to count the votes.

A computer program that was specially enhanced to speed the November 1993 Kane County, Illinois, election results to a waiting public did just that—unfortunately, it sped the wrong data. Voting totals for a dozen Illinois races were incomplete, and in one case they suggested that a local referendum proposal had lost when it actually had been approved. For some reason, software that had worked earlier without a hitch had waited until election night to omit eight precincts in the tally.

A squeaker—no, a landslide—oops, we reversed the totals—and about those absentee votes, make that 72-19, not 44–47. Software programming errors, sorry. Oh, and reverse that election, we announced the wrong winner. In the 2002 Clay County, Kansas, commissioner primary, voting machines said Jerry Mayo ran a close race but lost, garnering 48 percent of the vote, but a hand recount revealed Mayo had won by a landslide, receiving 76 percent of the vote.

Apparently voting machine miscounts have been taking place for some time. In a 1971 race in Las Vegas, Nevada, machines declared Democrat Arthur Espinoza to be the winner of a seat on the city assembly, but Republican Hal Smith challenged the election when he determined that some votes had not been counted because of a faulty voting machine. After unrecorded votes were tallied, Smith was declared the winner.

Flawed Excuses

The excuses given for these miscounts are just as flawed as the election results themselves. Vendors have learned that reporters and election workers will believe pretty much anything, as long as it sounds high-tech. They blame incorrect vote counts on "a bad chip" or "a faulty memory card," but defective chips and bad memory cards have very different symptoms. They don't function at all, or they spit out nonsensical data.

In the November 2002 general election in Scurry County, Texas, poll workers got suspicious about a landslide victory for two Republican commissioner candidates. Told that a "bad chip" was to blame, they had a new computer chip flown in and also counted the votes by hand—and found out that Democrats actually had won by wide margins, overturning the election.

We usually don't get an explanation for these miscounts. In 1986 the wrong candidate was declared the winner in Georgia. Incumbent Democrat Donn Peevy was running for state senator in District 48. The machines said he lost the election. After an investigation revealed that a Republican elections official had kept uncounted ballots in the trunk of his car, officials also admitted that a computerized voting program had miscounted. Peevy insisted on a recount. According to the *Atlanta Journal-Constitution*: "When the count finished around 1 a.m., they [the elections board] walked into a room and shut the door," recalls Peevy. "When they came out, they said, 'Mr. Peevy, you won.' That was it. They never apologized. They never explained."

> *Vendors have learned that reporters and election workers will believe pretty much anything, as long as it sounds high-tech.*

In a Seminole Nation election held in Oklahoma in August 1997, electronic voting machines gave the election to the wrong candidates twice. The private company hired to handle the election announced results for tribal chief and assistant chief, then decided that its computer had counted the absentee ballots twice. So the company posted a second set of results. Tribal officials then counted the votes by hand, producing yet a third, and this time official, set of results. A different set of candidates moved on to the runoff election each time.

If you insist on the right to vote for whom you want (and no one's gonna stop you), does it make a difference if misprogramming, rather than a human being, forces you to vote for someone you *don't* want?

News reports often explain miscounts as "software programming errors," with no follow-up and certainly no outrage. Yet incorrect programming is more insidious than Mad Myrtle secretly stuffing the ballot box. At least when we vote on paper ballots, hand counted, we can hold someone accountable. We don't even know the names of our voting machine programmers.

A software programming error gave the election to the wrong candidate in November 1999 in Onondaga County, New York. Bob Faulkner, a political newcomer, went to bed on election night confident he had helped complete a Republican sweep of three open council seats. But after Onondaga County Board of Elections staffers rechecked the totals, Faulkner had lost to Democratic incumbent Elaine Lytel. Just a few hours later, election officials discovered that a software programming error had given too many absentee ballot votes to Lytel. Faulkner took the lead. . . .

Despite Claims, Machines Are Inaccurate

Voting machine vendors claim these things are amazingly accurate. Bob Urosevich, who has headed three different voting machine companies under five different corporate names, said in 1990 that his company's optical-scan machines had an error rate of only "one-thousandth of 1 percent."

At that time, Urosevich was with ES&S (then called American Information Systems). Recently, the same Urosevich (now president of Diebold Election Systems, formerly called Global Election Systems) gave an even more glowing endorsement of his company's touch-screen accuracy.

"Considering the magnitude of these elections, which includes more than 870,000 registered voters within the four Maryland counties, we are very pleased with the results as every single vote was accurately counted," he said.

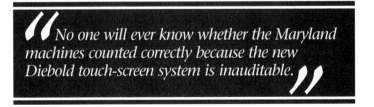

No one will ever know whether the Maryland machines counted correctly because the new Diebold touch-screen system is inauditable.

When Chuck Hagel accepted his position as chairman of American Information Systems, he offered a rousing endorsement: "The AIS system is 99.99 percent accurate," he assured us.

But do these claims hold up?

According to *The Wall Street Journal*, in the 2000 general election an optical-scan machine in Allamakee County, Iowa, was fed 300 ballots and reported 4 million votes. The county auditor tried the machine again but got the same result. Eventually, the machine's manufacturer, ES&S, agreed to have replacement equipment sent. Republicans had hoped that the tiny but heavily Republican county would tip the scales in George W. Bush's favor, but tipping it by almost four million votes attracted national attention.

These are real miscounts by voting machines, which took place in real elections.

"We don't have four million voters in the state of Iowa," said Bill Roe Jr., county auditor.

Todd Urosevich of ES&S said, "You are going to have some failures."

November 2003: Boone County, Indiana, officials wanted to know why their MicroVote machines counted 144,000 votes cast when only 5,352 existed.

"I about had a heart attack," said County Clerk Lisa Garofolo, according to the *Indianapolis Star*. "Believe me, there was nobody more shook up than I was."

If you are an elections official, I hope this litany gives you pause. Do you really need this kind of stress?

A Litany of Errors

With computerized voting, the certified and sworn officials step aside and let technicians, and sometimes the county computer guy, tell us the election results. The Boone County information technology director and a few MicroVote techs "fixed the problem." (For voting, I prefer the term "corrected.")

Better than a pregnant chad [produced by low-tech punch card ballots]—these machines can actually give birth.

In the 1996 McLennan County, Texas, Republican primary runoff, one precinct tallied about 800 votes, although only 500 ballots had been ordered. "It's a mystery," declared Elections Administrator Linda Lewis. Like detectives on the Orient Express, officials pointed fingers at one suspected explanation after another. One particular machine may have been the problem, Lewis said. That is, the miscounted votes were scattered throughout the precincts with no one area being miscounted more than another, Lewis also explained. Wait—some ballots may have been counted more than once, almost doubling the number of votes actually cast. Aha! That could explain it. (Er . . . excuse me, exactly *which* ballots were counted twice?)

"We don't think it's serious enough to throw out the election," said county Republican Party Chairman M.A. Taylor. Error size: 60 percent.

Here's a scorching little 66 percent error rate: Eight hundred twenty-six votes in one Tucson, Arizona-area precinct simply evaporated, remaining unaccounted for a month after the 1994 general election. No recount appears to have been done, even though two-thirds of voters did not get their votes counted. Election officials said the vanishing votes were the result of a faulty computer program. Apparently, the software programming error and the person who caused it are still at large.

Some voters aren't so sure that *every single vote* was accurately counted during the 2002 general election in Maryland.

According to the *Washington Times*, Kevin West of Upper Marlboro, who voted at the St. Thomas Church in Croom, said, "I pushed a Republican ticket for governor and his name disappeared. Then the Democrat's name got an 'X' put in it."

No one will ever know whether the Maryland machines counted correctly because the new Diebold touch-screen system is unauditable.

Problems from Dallas to Venezuela

Tom Eschberger became a vice president of ES&S not long after he accepted an immunity deal for cooperating with prosecutors in a case against Arkansas Secretary of State Bill McCuen, who pleaded guilty to taking kickbacks and bribes in a scheme related to computerized voting systems.

Eschberger reported that a test conducted on a malfunctioning machine and its software in the 1998 general election in Honolulu, Hawaii, showed the machine worked normally. He said the company did not know that the machine wasn't functioning properly until the Supreme Court ordered a recount, when a second test on the same machine detected that it wasn't counting properly.

"But again, in all fairness, there were 7,000 machines in Venezuela and 500 machines in Dallas that did not have problems," he said.

Really?

Dallas, Texas: A software programming error caused Dallas

County, Texas's new, $3.8 million high-tech ballot system to miss 41,015 votes during the November 1998 election. The system refused to count votes from 98 precincts, telling itself they already had been counted. Operators and election officials didn't realize they had a problem until after they'd released "final" totals that omitted one in eight votes.

In one of the nonsensical answers that we see so often from vendors, ES&S assured us that votes were never lost, just uncounted.

The company took responsibility and was trying to find two apparently unrelated software bugs, one that mistakenly indicated precinct votes were in when they weren't, and another that forgot to include 8,400 mail-in ballots in the final tally. Democrats were livid and suspicious, but Tom Eschberger said, "What we had was a speed bump along the way."

Caracas, Venezuela: In May 2000, Venezuela's highest court suspended elections because of problems with the vote tabulation for the national election. Venezuela sent an air force jet to Omaha to fetch experts from ES&S in a last-ditch effort to fix the problem. Dozens of protesters chanted, "Gringos get out!" at ES&S technicians. Venezuelan President Hugo Chavez accused ES&S of trying to destabilize the country's electoral process. Chavez asked for help from the U.S. government because, he said, the U.S. had recommended ES&S.

By Accident or by Design

Some people, when you give them the short but horrifying version of the electronic voting issue, insist on minimizing the problem. You tell them about an election that lost 25 percent of its votes, and they say, "That's just an isolated incident." When you add that another election had a 100 percent error, they call it a "glitch." When you tell them a voting machine was videotaped recording votes for the opposite candidate than the one selected, they say, "There are problems in every election."

No. We are not talking about a few minor glitches. These are real miscounts by voting machines, which took place in real elections. Almost all of them were caused by incorrect programming, whether by accident or by design. . . .

For the third time in as many elections, Pima County, Arizona, found errors in its tallies. The computers recorded no votes for 24 precincts in the 1998 general election, but voter rolls showed thousands had voted at those polling places. Pima was using Global Election Systems machines, which now are sold under the Diebold company name.

Officials in Broward County, Florida, had said that all the precincts were included in the Nov. 5, 2002, election and that the new, unauditable ES&S touch-screen machines had counted the vote without a major hitch. The next day, the County Elections Office discovered 103,222 votes had not been counted.

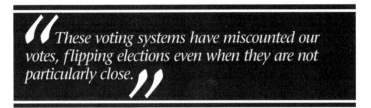

These voting systems have miscounted our votes, flipping elections even when they are not particularly close.

Allow me to shed some perspective on this. Do you remember when we got excited about a missing ballot box found in a Dade County, Florida, church day-care center in the 2000 presidential election? One hundred and three thousand uncounted votes represents about 1,000 ballot boxes. Broward Deputy Elections Supervisor Joe Cotter called the mistake "a minor software thing."

If you are a candidate, you know that participating even in a small election means raising or borrowing money, passing out flyers, going door to door and standing in the rain at various events. How do you feel if your vote is not counted accurately?

"I knew something was wrong when I looked up the results in my own precinct and it showed zero votes," said Illinois Democrat Rafael Rivera, according to the *Chicago Tribune*. "I said, 'Wait a minute. I know I voted for myself.'"

The problem cropped up during the Lake County, Illinois, election held April 1, 2003. Clerk Willard Helander blamed the problem on ES&S, the Omaha company in charge of operating Waukegan's optical-scan voting machines. Rivera said he felt as if he were living an episode of *The Twilight Zone*. No votes showed up for him, not even his own.

"It felt like a nightmare," he said.

Is this not alarming? These voting systems have miscounted our votes, flipping elections even when they are not particularly close. Even more alarming: We have no idea how many miscounts go unnoticed.

No legal authority permits privately employed technicians —often temporary workers—who are not sworn and don't work for the elections office, who sometimes are not even residents of the U.S., to determine the results of the election when there are discrepancies. Yet they do.

Ten days after the November 2002 election, Richard Romero, a Bernalillo County, New Mexico, Democrat, noticed that 48,000 people had voted early on unauditable Sequoia touch-screen computers, but only 36,000 votes had been tallied—a 25 percent error. Sequoia vice president Howard Cramer apologized for not mentioning that the same problem had happened before in Clark County, Nevada. A "software patch" was installed . . . , and Sequoia technicians in Denver *e-mailed* the "correct" results.

Not only did Cramer fail to mention to Bernalillo County that the problem had happened before in Nevada—just four months later, Sequoia salespersons also failed to mention it while making a sales presentation to Santa Clara County, California. A Santa Clara official tried to jog their memory. According to the minutes of this meeting, "Supervisor McHugh asked one of the vendors about a statistic saying there was a 25 percent error rate. . . . No one knew where this number came from and Sequoia said it was incorrect."

That meeting was held Feb. 11, 2003. Just 20 days before, in Snohomish County, Washington, at a meeting called because Sequoia optical-scan machines had failed to record 21 percent of the absentee votes, I asked about the 25 percent error in Bernalillo County. The Sequoia representative was well aware of the problem, replying quickly that *that* 25 percent error was caused by something quite different from *this* 21 percent problem. OK. *Nothing to see here—move along.*

6

Fears About Electronic Voting Machines Are Greatly Exaggerated

John Fund

John Fund is a columnist for the Wall Street Journal*'s OpinionJournal.com. He has written about election fraud for the* Wall Street Journal, *the* New Republic, *and other publications.*

Critics of electronic voting machines claim that balloting computers can be easily programmed to favor certain candidates. However, these conspiracy theorists have a limited knowledge of electronics as well as of elections. To perpetrate election fraud on a large scale using direct-recording electronic (DRE) machines would require the cooperation of dozens of computer technicians, politicians, and election officials. The odds are small that so many would commit felonies in order to support their candidate. While DREs are subject to glitches and mistakes, they are much more accurate than the old-fashioned voting machines they have replaced. DREs are here to stay, and those promoting dark political conspiracies should be happy that their votes are being recorded on safe, accurate machines.

With the exception of the 2000 Florida fiasco [in the presidential race between Al Gore and George W. Bush], the biggest collection of conspiracy theories about our national elections centers around the direct-recording electronic machines (DREs) that thirty-five million Americans . . . [used] to record their votes in November 2004.

These machines are designed to remedy the chads and dimples and butterfly ballots that made voting for president so chaotic in Florida during the 2000 election. In an effort to design a new system . . . many states, including Florida and its neighbor Georgia, have installed DREs, which instantly record and tabulate votes. Some even use fancy touch-screen technology similar to automated teller machines in banks. But the machines have become the latest punching bag in the mutual war of suspicion over which side is trying to steal elections.

It is necessary to put the paranoia about computer voting into perspective by remembering that every election system is subject to fraud and errors. Paper ballots were so abused in the nineteenth century that lever voting machines were developed. Bosses in Chicago and other places soon learned how to add votes by turning the wheels at the back of the machine, leaving no evidence of their handiwork. The punch-card machines and optical scanners that replaced these lever machines in the 1960s in many places had problems with the subjective reading of improperly filled-out ballots; and as we've already seen in abundant detail, ballots could easily be altered or voided while they were transported to a central counting station.

Problems Have Been Fixed

As the latest technology, DREs bring with them a separate set of concerns. Some computer scientists are alarmed by the possibility that unscrupulous programmers could manipulate the new machines. Internal documents from Diebold Election Systems, which has sold more than 33,000 touch-screen DRE machines, acknowledge that there have been security flaws, although the company denies that these flaws could allow a hacker to cast multiple votes or alter the votes of others, as some critics of the new technology suggest. Diebold insists that the problems have been or are being fixed, but the company is haunted by the perception (in part created preemptively by Democratic operatives) that Walden O'Dell, the chairman and CEO of Diebold (and a major Bush contributor), is a Republican stooge planning to use his company's software to tilt the election count. O'Dell's activism and six-figure contributions by Diebold to Republicans have set off a frenzy of conspiracy chat on the Internet.

Bev Harris, a 52-year-old freelance journalist from Seattle, has led a crusade against the new technology ever since she learned that Georgia had become the first state to replace all its old machines with shiny new DREs from Diebold. She became convinced that the results of the Georgia Senate race lost by incumbent Democrat Max Cleland in 2002 were suspect. Her only evidence was that Cleland had led in the final pre-election poll by five points but wound up losing by seven. (Cleland himself says the campaign against him was dirty, but acknowledges that he lost fairly. He says it's a good thing Georgia led the nation in adopting statewide electronic voting.)

> *Any Democrat who thinks that getting rid of direct electronic voting machines will help the Democrats win is simply out to lunch.*

But through her sleuthing Harris did turn up some gold when, in surfing the Internet, she happened upon 40,000 unprotected computer files owned by Diebold. The Internet files included material on its Global Election Management System tabulation software, source codes for Diebold's AccuVote touchscreen voting machine, a Texas voter registration list, and live vote data from fifty-seven precincts in a 2002 California primary election.

Harris also learned from her perusal of the files that Diebold machines sold to the State of Georgia could be accessed with a "supervisor smart card" and that every one of the 22,000 machines had the same entry password: 1111. State officials had the machines tested by two independent labs, which approved them. But Harris questions how independent the labs are since one of them gave $25,000 to the Republican National Committee in 2000.

Out of these facts and factoids was born a conspiracy theory that is bound to grow in magnitude and influence because so much of our overall electoral system is indeed in a sorry state.

A Democrat Punctures the Conspiracy Balloon

Joe Andrew was chairman of the Democratic National Committee until [President] Bill Clinton left office in 2001. He is also the only chairman of a national political party who has ever come from a technology background, having been a partner in a biotechnology firm that owned several Internet companies. He considers himself a Democrat with a foot in both the party establishment and the growing progressive movement that congregated around [2004 presidential candidate] Howard Dean. "I own both an Oldsmobile and a Blackberry," he jokes.

But Andrew says the conspiracy theories surrounding electronic voting are no laughing matter. In June 2004 he gave a speech to the Maryland Association of Election Officials that ripped the bark off the "black box" conspiracy theorists. "When it comes to electronic voting, most liberals are just plain old-fashioned nuts," he told the election officials. While conservatives were skilled at coordinating their messages and agendas, "that does not mean there is a vast right-wing conspiracy trying to steal votes in America, as the loudest voices on the left are saying today."

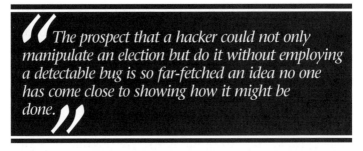

The prospect that a hacker could not only manipulate an election but do it without employing a detectable bug is so far-fetched an idea no one has come close to showing how it might be done.

Andrew divided the people who were obsessed about a DRE stolen election into two groups: computer experts with impressive technical experience but little practical experience with elections, and progressive computer users who are conspiratorial by nature. He claims they have been joined in their hysteria by the Democratic Party and prominent members of Congress who "are rallying behind the anti-DRE bandwagon in a big election year because they think that this movement is good for Democrats."

Sadly, he says the people they are hurting are mostly Democrats. "Any Democrat who thinks that getting rid of direct electronic voting machines will help the Democrats win is simply out to lunch," he told the election officials. He noted that the Leadership Conference on Civil Rights has generally supported electronic voting because study after study has found that the voters who are most likely to be helped by DREs are:

a) the disabled (they can vote without assistance); b) the less-educated (the machines resemble the ubiquitous ATM); c) lower socioeconomic groups (who often trust machines more than people); d) the truly elderly (you can increase the type size) and citizens more comfortable voting in a language other than English.

Indeed, as many problems as DREs have, they must be assessed in comparison with the other existing systems. In California's 2003 recall election, . . . punch-card systems failed to record a valid vote on 6.3 percent of all ballots cast. For optical scan systems, the rate was 2.7 percent, and for DREs the rate was only 1.5 percent. If accuracy was our only goal, then DREs were almost twice as accurate as the next available technology.

As for the theories about how DREs could be programmed to change an election, Andrew maintained that "it is not possible to move a constant fraction of votes from one party to another in each jurisdiction without it being obvious that something is going on." He concluded that "the liberal Internet activists are bonkers."

Or maybe not. By whipping up a frenzy of suspicion about electronic voting, Democrats will have built a platform from which . . . they can launch endless lawsuits everywhere there were problems with electronic machines. . . .

Inside the Black Box

Direct-recording electronic machines are polarizing gadgets. One side sees a security and reliability nightmare. . . . Including suspicions that these "black boxes" will either add or eat votes depending on which candidate some "Manchurian Programmer" wants to win. The other side sees DREs as the most modern machines available, offering a significantly lower rate of ballot spoilage than other technologies, including paper.

As for security, the source code used to program any machine can be open for inspection to enough people that any anomaly will be caught. Most importantly, the machines are *not* hooked up to the Internet; they are stand-alone machines. "Hackers can do anything only in books and movies," says Michael Shamos, a professor of computer science at Carnegie Mellon University who served as Pennsylvania's examiner of electronic voting systems for twenty years. "The prospect that a hacker could not only manipulate an election but do it without employing a detectable bug is so far-fetched an idea no one has come close to showing how it might be done."

There certainly are problems with DREs that demand attention. Some of the voting machine companies that produce them have dubious records of competence or integrity, and demand more scrutiny by both the media and election officials. Some states have rushed to buy new equipment that they don't know how to operate, and they didn't insist on getting a copy of the computer software used in the machines. Many devices will inevitably break down . . . and cause long lines, unhappy voters and even more conspiracy theories.

But breakdowns don't equal conspiracy. Susan Zevin, the former deputy director of the Commerce Department's National Institute of Standards and Technology, says there is "absolutely no evidence" that an election has been altered by fraud in an electronic system. The nightmare scenarios conjured up by Harris and her Internet allies can be completely prevented if the machines are rigorously tested by outsiders. Zevin says the computer experts who side with Harris are very knowledgeable but have almost zero experience in election administration. "It's easy in a laboratory to write a program that throws an election," she notes, "but you don't have elections in a laboratory."

Most electronic voting machines transfer the election results to a compact disk or some other "read only" format. These CDs are then taken to a central location where they are read into a computer. Breaking into each machine one at a time without breaking the tamper-proof seals and being detected is possible but highly unlikely. In the twenty-plus years that these machines have been used, in many counties all across the country, there has never been a verified case of tampering.

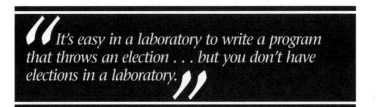

It's easy in a laboratory to write a program that throws an election . . . but you don't have elections in a laboratory.

What about the nightmare scenario that Diebold's Walden O'Dell will secretly program the computers to alter the election results? Audit devices and parallel testing regimes should accompany any machine to make sure any such manipulation is caught. Professor Shamos says "the manipulations of any vendor can be made fruitless if we separate the candidate and party names from the capture and recording logic of the computer program. A vendor or hacker won't know who he is helping or hurting."

If Republicans can be fearful of union bosses manipulating votes in back-room boiler operations then they should sympathize if Democrats fear geeky Republican hackers in the back rooms of computer companies.

It's true that in Maryland, computer experts hired by election officials to test the security of the state's individual Diebold machines easily hacked into the DREs, either directly or through telephone lines. The machines failed the test completely. Yet the tampering wasn't under real-world conditions. An old system was used, and although the hackers succeeded in their break-in, the original data in the voting machines were not compromised; in the real world it would still have been possible to conduct an accurate recount.

Overstating the Vulnerability

Britain J. Williams, a retired professor of computer science who has spent eighteen years evaluating computer-based voting systems for the State of Georgia, says the critics overstate the vulnerability of election systems to manipulation because they ignore the many safeguards in place. They would be better off focusing on the many sloppy software errors and poorly trained election workers that do indeed tarnish the track record of many DREs.

Still, it is worth noting that the DRE conspiracy theorists have very little to say about its close cousin, the optical scan machine in which a voter fills in a circle next to his choice and has the ballot read by a scanner. Optical scan machines present at least as many if not more security concerns because, unlike DREs, they do use a central computer. But people have employed optical scanners for decades. They are old hat and people wouldn't believe wild claims about them. New technology always carries with it the fear of the unknown; hence the "black box" label that Bev Harris has tacked onto DREs.

Despite the misplaced hysteria, it is still probably a good idea to move toward a voter-verified paper record of each ballot. Representative Rush Holt (D-NJ) has a bill to require such a paper trail for every DRE and has 106 sponsors. Representative Steve King (R-IA) has a simpler bill with fewer extraneous federal mandates for the states. Roman Buhler, a former Republican staffer for the House Administration Committee, advised King on his bill. He admits that if "Republicans can be fearful of union bosses manipulating votes in back-room boiler operations then they should sympathize if Democrats fear geeky Republican hackers in the back rooms of computer companies. The fear is mostly illegitimate, but public confidence is important."

Indeed, perception is everything. People get paper reassurance that their money is safely and accurately counted every time they use an ATM. A "voter-verified" paper trail means that, before completing the voting process, voters can examine a paper printout of their choices, under glass. This allows officials to perform a manual recount later on if there is an electronic failure.

But paper ballot records are infinitely longer than ATM receipts; they present storage problems and require heavy-duty printers that won't break down and cause chaos at a polling place. More reliable printers and new machines with verified paper trails are slowly heading for the market. . . .

The price of progress is eternal vigilance about its risks. This is why it's important that we realize that DREs, along with every other new technology, can have security and accuracy problems. This doesn't mean that the technology is unworkable, but that the problems have to be squarely addressed and not swept under the rug, as some of the voting machine companies have seemed eager to do.

Felons Who Have Served Their Time Should Be Allowed to Vote

Elizabeth Hull

Elizabeth Hull is an associate professor of political science at Rutgers University who has written extensively on the constitutional rights of noncitizens and racial minorities. Hull is the author of two books: Without Justice for All: The Constitutional Rights of Aliens, *and* Taking Liberties: National Barriers to the Free Flow of Ideas.

Millions of people who have committed felonies are permanently barred from voting in most states. These people, many of whom are minorities, have finished their prison sentences and have paid their debt to society. Yet their disenfranchisement lasts a lifetime, even if their crime was as relatively minor as using false identification, intentionally writing bad checks, or selling small quantities of drugs. Laws that prevent felons from voting have long been used to repress the minority vote. These restrictions are antiquated and racist and should be repealed so that all citizens can be fairly represented by their government.

In the 2000 presidential election, one of 50 U.S. adult citizens —4,200,000 nationwide—were ineligible to vote. These disempowered Americans are former convicts, men and women who have completed their sentences, paroles, and the terms of probation but still are prohibited by many state laws from casting a ballot. In a country that has extended voting privileges to virtually every other class of citizen, members of this group are deemed unworthy to exercise what the Supreme Court has labeled "the right preservative of all other rights." Unfortunately for ex-prisoners, Article 2 of the 14th Amendment permits states to deny voting privileges to anyone found guilty of "rebellion or other serious crimes."

> *The policy [of stripping voting rights from felons] creates what Human Rights Watch calls 'a huge pool of political outcasts in America.'*

On Dec. 9, 2000, in *Bush v. Gore*, the Supreme Court halted a presidential ballot recount under way in Florida because, it said, the standards being used to determine "voter intent" differed from county to county, thereby denying the state's residents their constitutional right to equal protection. This inconsistence is virtually inconsequential, however, compared to the disparate treatment former inmates receive throughout the country when they attempt to vote. Forty-eight states and the District of Columbia restrict the voting rights of felons in some manner. The lone exceptions are Maine and Vermont. Thirty-two states bar parolees from voting, and 2) forbid anyone on probation from casting a ballot. While many states automatically reenfranchise felons once they are released from prison, 14 others effectively prohibit even those who have "paid their debts" from ever voting again. Alabama, for example, imposes a lifetime ban whether the individual is convicted of a Federal or state offense, whereas Arizona and Maryland do so following a second felony conviction. In Tennessee, it affects only those whose offenses occurred before 1986, and in Washington state the ban applies to individuals whose crimes took place before 1984.

Among the states, moreover, what constitutes a felony is neither logical nor consistent. In Maryland, for instance, criminals cannot vote for the rest of their lives if they are twice convicted of a felony (or what the state calls "infamous crimes"). Yet, many of the 149 offenses so categorized—such as inserting slugs into a slot machine or using a false identification card—are regarded in other states as misdemeanors. Any Floridian who stops payment on a check of more than $150 with intent to defraud commits a felony; so does the teenager who is caught with an ounce of crack cocaine, but the recreational user who is nabbed for cocaine (in powder form) possession is guilty of a misdemeanor.

Such wildly divergent policies defy the move toward "uniform national standards" that an election-reform commission, prompted by the Court's ruling in *Bush v. Gore*, urged upon the country. There is another, even more important reason why stripping voting rights from former inmates is objectional: The policy creates what Human Rights Watch calls "a huge pool of political outcasts in America." The organization further indicates that it knows "of no other country in the world that permanently disenfranchises ex-offenders." Indeed, many other liberal, democratic nations, including Germany, France, and, most recently, South Africa, extend the franchise even to individuals still behind bars. Yet, in some regions of the U.S., as Florida State Sen. Delores Kelly observes, "If you write two bad checks over $500, you [could] lose your right in perpetuity to be a part of the body politic."

The disenfranchisement of felons would be less alarming, perhaps, if there were fewer of them. The U.S., however, is second only to Russia in the number of people behind bars. This country incarcerates, proportionately, anywhere from five to eight times more individuals than any other industrialized nation. Starting in 1973, the U.S. has witnessed an unprecedented rise in prison population among democracies. In 1973, there were 200,000 people in prison; at the conclusion of 2000, there were 10 times that number.

Minorities Disenfranchised

According to U.S. government statistics two-thirds of those imprisoned are members of racial and ethnic minorities. Not surprisingly, then, among those who are disenfranchised, 36% are African-American. The degree of restrictions affecting minorities varies among states. The Sentencing Project, a prisoner advocacy group based in Washington, D.C., reports that one of every three adult black men is barred for life from voting in the state of Alabama, and, in another eight states, the figure is one in five. In 17 other states, anywhere from 10 to 25% of black men have lost their political suffrage. Given the number of African-American youth who are in prison, as much as 40% of black men will be denied the vote during some or all of their adult lives. This massive disenfranchisement is wreaking havoc on many minority communities by sapping political power from a group whose influence in legislative corridors already is slight.

Since some disenfranchisement laws were enacted as far back as the colonial period, their advocates insist they are non-racist in origin. Indeed, according to historian Malcolm McMillan, some early laws were not intended to handicap racial minorities (who could not vote in any case), but to dilute the strength of land-poor whites and "legally create a conservative electorate." Yet, as The League of Women Voters points out in a 2001 newsletter, many others "are anachronistic remnants of the hideous post–Civil War Reconstruction period." The majority of disenfranchisement laws were enacted between 1865–70, along with poll taxes and literacy tests, to ensure white supremacy. As Sen. Carter Glass (D-Va., 1920–46) made clear, these measures were intended "to discriminate to the very extremity of permissible action under the limits of the Federal Constitution, with a view to the elimination of every Negro voter who can be gotten rid of legally, without materially impairing the numerical strength of the white electorate."

> *One of every three adult black men is barred for life from voting in the state of Alabama, and, in another eight states, the figure is one in five.*

Laws disempowering blacks were pivotal, historian Morgan Kousser explains, because they provided southern states with "insurance if courts struck down the more blatantly unconstitutional clauses." This insurance worked as intended. While the Supreme Court eventually banned literacy tests and poll taxes, it never has overturned the constitutionality of laws that deny political rights to former convicts. In their campaign to eviscerate blacks' voting strength, Reconstructionist Southerners also designated as felonies all sorts of offenses, such as "horse theft" "public rowdiness," that racial minorities presumably were more likely to commit than whites. Miscegenation became a felony as well. As a consequence, for the next half-century, people could murder and rape without losing the franchise, but if they married someone of another race, they forfeited their voting rights into perpetuity.

According to Florida State Sen. Daryl Jones, 'The state legislature attempts to classify more and more crimes as felonies [so it] can eliminate more people from the voter rolls.'

Even in the present era, according to Florida State Sen. Daryl Jones, "The state legislature attempts to classify more and more crimes as felonies [so it] can eliminate more people from the voter rolls." In 2000, Jones reports, the Republican legislature proposed a bill that would have increased from 365 to 366 days the jail sentence for anyone who cashes two welfare checks after gaining employment. What is the purpose of adding one more day? The offense then becomes a felony, and "You take one more person off the voter rolls. . . . It's been going on in Tallahassee for years."

Under Alabama law, "moral turpitude" also was classified as a felony. (In 1985, the Supreme Court invalidated the statute, concluding that since 10 times as many blacks as whites had lost their voting rights in the years subsequent to its adoption, the statute represented an attempt "to disenfranchise practically all of the African-Americans.")

Obstacles to Voting

In many states, disenfranchised ex-convicts can petition for the reinstatement of their political rights—in theory. In reality, regaining the franchise is almost always a lengthy, tortuous, costly, demeaning, and frustrating endeavor. Elsewhere, former inmates must wait several years after their release before they can even seek the restoration of their political rights. In Nevada, it is 10 years, in Virginia, five (unless they were convicted on drug charges, in which case it is seven). In other states, one-time felons cannot regain their right to vote until they have paid a hefty application fee—in Florida, as much as $1,000. In Alabama, the pardon-seeker must take a DNA test and notify the crime victim and then seek and be granted a pardon from both the governor and a clemency panel (or, if the applicant has been in Federal prison, from the president of the U.S.). Predictably, few succeed. In Virginia, for instance, in 1996–97, 404 out of some 200,000 eligible were granted clemency. In 1999, one out of every 300 ex-convicts regained the vote in Florida—less than one-half of one percent of those eligible. (Among them was Charles Colson, who was incarcerated for his involvement in the 1972 Watergate scandal.)

No Clear Purpose

Disenfranchisement laws, for all their inequities, remain widespread. Their proponents argue that they promote important social goals. For example, it is claimed that they further one or more of the traditional objectives of the criminal justice system: deterrence, restitution, rehabilitation, or punishment. Yet, denying voting privileges to former inmates scarcely furthers these legitimate objectives. There is no evidence it deters crime, and it strains credulity to assume would-be felons will refrain from burgling a store, say, or selling drugs lest they jeopardize their franchise. Denying the vote does not compensate crime victims, and certainly does nothing to promote the rehabilitation of people who have "paid their debt" to society. Disenfranchising a person, sometimes for life, does indeed constitute punishment. Yet besides the fact such a policy seems mindlessly punitive, whom is it harming? Not those hardened offenders who could not care less about voting. Instead, it hurts those ex-convicts who, upon serving their time, live a law-abiding life and participate in civil society.

No less a conservative than James Q. Wilson, who ranks among the country's foremost criminologists, concedes that a "perpetual loss of the right to vote serves no practical or philosophical purpose." Even if disenfranchisement laws did serve some legitimate law enforcement objective, there is no correspondence between the punishment and the crime. Confiscating the license of someone convicted of drunk driving is just. So does forbidding a scam artist from working in a bank. However, prohibiting an embezzler or arsonist from ever casting a ballot makes as much sense as forbidding a stock swindler from coaching Little League.

Those supporting disenfranchisement laws defend them on another ground as well: Such laws are necessary, they maintain, because ex-prisoners as a class are likely to corrupt the electoral process. Those living in sparsely populated regions could determine the outcome of close elections, particularly in jurisdictions where the populace directly elects judges, law enforcement officials, and district attorneys. Law-and-order sheriffs might not be reelected if every former inmate they had sent away resolved to vote for their opponents. Lawbreakers might collude to steal property, but it is hard to believe they would join together to steal ballots. Such an allegation assumes that, upon their release, they will plunge headlong into the political arena to bribe candidates or otherwise rig the outcome. Virtually every study on voting behavior indicates that most lawbreakers are marginalized and politically apathetic—the least inclined sector to vote. In Massachusetts, for instance, only 25% of those entering prison had voted previously, and, in Utah, less than five percent even had registered.

> *Prohibiting an embezzler or arsonist from ever casting a ballot makes as much sense as forbidding a stock swindler from coaching Little League.*

Neither is there any substantiation that former prisoners corrupt the political process. Indeed, the 20 states that allow them to vote experience no more election-related corruption than the 30 that do not. Even if corruption is a genuine concern, there are more appropriate ways to safeguard the integrity of the electoral process. Why not just strip the franchise from those few miscreants whose offenses affected the casting or counting of ballots?

Voting as a Privilege

Finally, disenfranchisement laws are necessary, their defenders insist, because former prisoners have shown themselves unworthy of exercising what Reg Brown, an attorney working for Florida Gov. Jeb Bush, describes as a "privilege, not a right." This prerogative is properly withheld not only because erstwhile prisoners have "broken the social compact," but because, in so doing, they have shown themselves either to be morally or mentally deficient. As a court in the 19th century explained, lawbreakers are like "idiots, insane persons and miners . . .

[who] lack the requisite judgment and discretion which fit them for the exercise."

Yet, if "competence" and "good moral character" were prerequisites, the number of individuals eligible to vote surely would plummet. Purists, for example, might exclude the 60% of Americans who, when polled, could not name the vice-president, along with anyone else who ever has received a speeding ticket or voted on the basis of blatant self-interest. Predicating eligibility on either "competence" or "moral worth," most importantly, would undermine the very foundation of democratic government, which is premised on, dedicated to, and legitimated by the principle that voting should be a near-universal right. Why? Because, as economist and philosopher John Stuart Mill explained in an 1861 essay, every adult citizen knows best what is in his or her interest: "Men, as well as women, do not need political rights in order that they may govern, but in order that they not be misgoverned."

New Mexico and Connecticut recently restored voting rights to felons subject to their discharge from prison. More changes may come in response to recommendations made by the National Commission on Federal Election Reform. Under the leadership of former presidents Jimmy Carter and Gerald Ford, it advocates restoring voting privileges to former prisoners. However, in Massachusetts and Utah, which until recently had been two of the four states allowing inmates to vote, citizens endorsed ballot initiatives repealing the privilege. In Florida, meanwhile, lawmakers passed a package of essential and long overdue ballot reforms, although they tabled a bill to expand the voting rights of former prisoners.

Is it fair to deny suffrage to people who have completed their prison terms? As Columbia University law professor George Fletcher observes, "The idea that you would pay the debt and be treated as a debtor (felon) forever verges on the macabre." Is it not a principle basic to Judeo-Christian ethics, and indeed a tenet underlying this country's criminal justice system, that individuals can atone for their sins and be redeemed? Disenfranchisement laws not only are unfair, they are undemocratic and injurious. They compromise the country's political legitimacy and its moral authority to exact obedience and loyalty from those it presumes to represent. They weaken the body politic by fostering an outlaw caste, heavily weighted with racial and ethnic minorities who already are ill-equipped to assume productive lives in American society. Why compound their disabilities by telling them they are unfit to exercise the privileges of citizenship?

On April 1, 1999, South Africa's highest court voted unanimously to extend voting rights to former prisoners. As it explained when announcing the decision, "The vote of each and every citizen is a hedge of dignity and personhood. Quite literally, everybody counts." The U.S. too, could honor its ideals by making sure that "everybody counts."

Felons Should Not Be Allowed to Vote

Christopher M. Tozzo

People who commit felonies can be forced to pay large fines, surrender their freedom, and even face the death penalty. Therefore, there is little reason felons should expect to retain their voting rights. Sexual predators, drug dealers, bank robbers, and murderers have caused lifelong suffering for others and deserve the lifetime punishment of losing their right to vote. While most felons eventually serve their time and are released from prison, society owes them nothing in return. The Constitution allows states to deny criminals the right to vote, and this punishment is the price that must be paid by those who break the law.

I'm sorry, but I refuse to get excited about the fact that felons can't vote:

On Election Day it will not matter to some 4.7 million Americans whether they are Republicans, Democrats, independents or whether they have an opinion on anything at all. Under various state laws, they are barred from voting because they have felony records. This includes not just prison inmates (48 states), parolees (33 states) and probationers (29 states) but also a large number of people—one third of the disenfranchised in all—who are off parole and "free." Minorities are hit particularly hard by these state laws: They deny 13 percent of African American men the vote.

The 14th Amendment permits states to deny the vote "for participation in rebellion, or other crime." And it can be argued

Christopher M. Tozzo, JD, CFA, "Red Felon, Blue Felon," www.kipesquire.com, August 14, 2004. Reproduced by permission of the author.

that prisoners should not vote; after all, the purpose of prison is to deny freedom. But with ex-cons, the argument shifts.

Another bald fact: Many disenfranchisement laws trace to the mid-1800s, when they were crafted to bar blacks with even minor criminal records from polls. Today this poisonous legal lineage tells not only in the South, which retains the most repressive statutes, but in states such as New York, where ex-parolees theoretically get their rights back but in reality encounter local election officials who demand discharge papers that don't exist, give misleading information and find other reasons to turn them away. A class-action lawsuit in New York charges that this system bars so many voters in high-crime neighborhoods that the districts effectively have lost their voice. In Florida, where many felons are barred forever unless the governor personally decides otherwise, 8 percent of adults cannot vote—including one in four black men.

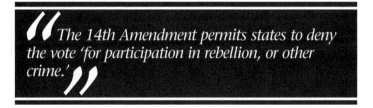

The 14th Amendment permits states to deny the vote 'for participation in rebellion, or other crime.'

Voting is not a privilege; it is the basic right that defines a citizen. Those denied it are, in effect, stateless—people without a country. This is not a partisan issue, but one of basic human rights. People who have paid their debt to society should have their rights restored.

Um, no.

Some Punishments Should Be Forever

It needs to be said: *the best way to empower felons is by not being one of them.* Of all the people one can have sympathy—misplaced or otherwise—toward, people are choosing felons? . . .

The notion that there should always be a final, definitive cut-off point for punishment, that there should always be some clearly-drawn line beyond which lies total forgiveness and forgetfulness, *simply has no basis either in the law or in common sense.* Some punishments are and should be forever, and there is nothing intrinsic to the franchise to suggest that denying felons the vote cannot be one of those lifetime punishments.

I'm an attorney—if I commit a great enough offense to my profession, then I can be disbarred for life. Same thing for my other day job as an investment banker—a lifetime ban from the securities industry is an all too common event on Wall Street. . . . People lose drivers licenses and other permits for life in certain circumstances. Countries can refuse people entry for life. We even *imprison* people for life if the crime is terrible enough. So what's the big deal about denying felons the right to vote?

Voting "defines a citizen"? I thought obeying the law and respecting the rights of others defined citizenship. To deny felons the vote is to deny them their rights? Didn't the felons themselves violate somebody's rights somewhere along the way, and might not the victims be suffering for life? Can't there be some "debts to society" that can never be totally repaid?

Certainly there may be specific instances of inconsistency or inappropriateness or flat-out abuse in the application of franchise denial to felons. But as a basic legal, political and philosophical question, there is simply no rational basis to oppose denying felons the franchise.

It's definitely fair . . . and it's probably wise.

Whether your true motivation is partisan politics, racial activism or a genuine concern for felons . . . your energies are better directed elsewhere. There are people more deserving of your efforts and more in need of "empowerment."

9

Illegal Aliens Should Not Be Allowed to Vote

Michelle Malkin

Michelle Malkin is a syndicated columnist and maintains a Web log at michellemalkin.com.

Every illegal alien living and working within the United States is doing so in violation of the law. Despite this fact, many Democrats want to give illegal aliens the right to vote, rather than deporting them for violating immigration laws. The motivation for these Democrats is to gain the illegal alien vote. In the post-9/11 world, granting the vote to illegal immigrants is ill-conceived and dangerous. With several known terrorists already shown to be on the voting rolls, Congress should work to ensure that illegal aliens cannot cast a vote in any election.

The right to vote is precious, the politicians preach. Our democracy hangs in the balance, the pundits screech.

Yes, but if we all value the sanctity of the voting process so highly, why is it that I've never once been asked to produce identification of any kind in the 16 years I've been a voter, from Ohio to California to Washington state to Maryland?

And why is it that we can't protect our elections from people who have no right to vote, no right to be here, and no right to undermine our safety or sovereignty?

While unhinged Democrats spread fear about the alleged discriminatory disenfranchisement of American citizens, they have supported the indiscriminate enfranchisement of untold numbers of foreign outlaws—including suspected al Qaeda op-

Michelle Malkin, "The Illegal Alien Swing Vote," www.townhall.com, October 27, 2004. Copyright © 2004 by Michelle Malkin and Creators Syndicate, Inc. Reproduced by permission.

eratives and terrorist sympathizers. . . .

[In October 2004], the *Columbus (Ohio) Dispatch* reported that illegal alien Nuradin Abdi—the suspected shopping mall bomb plotter from Somalia—was registered to vote in the battleground state of Ohio by the Association of Community Organizations for Reform Now (ACORN), a left-wing activist group. Also on the Ohio voting rolls: convicted al Qaeda agent Iyman Faris, who planned to sabotage the Brooklyn Bridge and had entered the country fraudulently from Pakistan on a student visa.

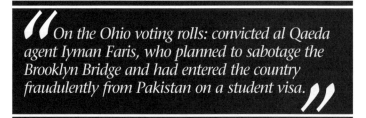

On the Ohio voting rolls: convicted al Qaeda agent Iyman Faris, who planned to sabotage the Brooklyn Bridge and had entered the country fraudulently from Pakistan on a student visa.

In the battleground state of Florida, indicted terror suspect Sami Al-Arian illegally cast his ballot in a Tampa referendum in 1994 while his citizenship application was pending. He claimed the unlawful vote was the result of a "misunderstanding." State officials declined to prosecute.

Hijackers Eligible to Vote

You've heard about those satirical "10 out of 10 terrorists agree: Anybody But Bush" bumper stickers? There may be more truth to them than you think. John Fund, author of *Stealing Elections: How Voter Fraud Threatens Our Democracy*, reports that at least eight of the 19 Sept. 11 hijackers were eligible to vote in Virginia or Florida while they plotted to kill Americans.

What's to stop the next foreign terrorist plotter from casting a tainted ballot in the nation he has sworn to destroy? Not much. According to the Franklin County Board of Elections, the *Dispatch* reports, the office simply "takes a person's word, that they're (sic) a U.S. citizen."

In the battleground state of Wisconsin, the story is the same for those who are responsible for registering other people to vote. Not only do we regularly do nothing to verify the citizenship of people voting, but we also shrug our shoulders at the citizenship status of election workers. I recently obtained a disturbing set of investigative reports from the Federation for

American Immigration Reform (FAIR), outlining how the city of Racine neglects to ask deputy registrar applicants for identification or proof of citizenship.

FAIR's investigation also alleges that a deputy registrar in Racine registered two individuals—one posing as an admitted illegal alien—and reportedly advised them to lie on their forms. The report notes that the deputy registrar—working for the open borders lobbying group, Voces de la Frontera—then gave the couple information on other illegal alien benefits, including employment rights and bank accounts.

Law enforcement officials in Wisconsin—which has been swamped with voter fraud shenanigans—have copies of the report, affidavits from the couple who dealt with the registrar and recordings of their conversations.

Democrats Seek the Votes of Illegal Aliens

Democrats at the state and federal levels have aggressively courted the illegal alien swing vote. The most egregious example, of course, was the taxpayer-funded Citizenship USA program under the Clinton-Gore administration, which abandoned criminal background checks to naturalize 1.3 million immigrants (including scores of criminal alien felons) in time for the 1996 elections.

Ethnic and racial grievance groups, with backing from the likes of [Democratic senators] Hillary Clinton and Ted Kennedy, have forcefully opposed basic ID requirements at the polls. And they have armies of lawyers standing by to assist them. Responsible election officials who ask for proof of citizenship will be accused of "harassment" and "intimidation." They will be accused of causing a "chilling effect"—never mind the corrosive effect of unchecked illegal alien voter fraud on law, order and the integrity of our electoral system.

10

Noncitizens Should Be Allowed to Participate in Elections

Joaquin Avila

Joaquin Avila is an expert on minority voting rights issues and former president of the Mexican American Legal Defense and Educational Fund.

Noncitizens make up more than half the population in some California cities. These people work, pay taxes, and send their children to local schools. Despite the contributions they make to their communities, noncitizens are denied the right to vote and the right to run for political office. It is unfair to deny political representation to more than four million noncitizens in California. It is also unhealthy for democracy for the state to be divided into two classes of people—those who are granted political rights and those who are not. Laws must be changed to allow noncitizens to participate in the electoral process. Joaquin Avila's policy brief encourages increasing public awareness about the continued political exclusion of noncitizen populations and highlights the benefits of noncitizen voting in order to create a more inclusive and unified society. The release of the report in December 2003 resulted in extensive media coverage and heated public debate.

Latino political empowerment has often been measured in terms of the increasing number of Latino elected officials or the elimination of discriminatory election structures. Today an-

Joaquin Avila, "Political Apartheid in California: Consequences of Excluding a Growing Noncitizen Population," *Latino Policy & Issues Brief no. 9*, December 2003. Copyright © 2003 by the Regents of the University of California, UCLA Chicano Studies Research Center. Reproduced by permission. Not for further reproduction.

other critical gauge of Latino political empowerment merits a renewed focus: the issue of noncitizens and voting. In California, over 4.6 million noncitizen adults—or nearly 19% of the adult population—contribute to the state economy and government revenues but lack political representation. Latino noncitizens account for 3 million of this noncitizen population and constitute 28% of Latinos in California. How we respond to these demographic changes will shape the future viability of [California] . . .

The Demographic Imperative

The 2000 U.S. Census data reveal that California has at least 85 cities where noncitizens comprise over 25% of the city's total adult population, and, remarkably, 12 municipalities where noncitizens comprise the majority (50–63%) of adults. Another 18 municipalities have noncitizen adult populations between 40 and 49%. Strikingly, in Los Angeles, the largest city in California, the noncitizen adult population share is approximately one-third of the population (32%). In other words, California state and local revenues, not to mention participation in community affairs, depend on a growing noncitizen population.

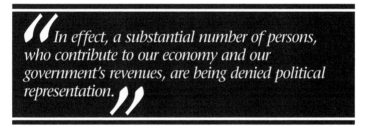

In effect, a substantial number of persons, who contribute to our economy and our government's revenues, are being denied political representation.

These statistics are alarming. In effect, a substantial number of persons, who contribute to our economy and our government's revenues, are being denied political representation. . . .

The Need for Political Integration

This trend is unfortunate. Efforts should be redirected toward the political integration of the immigrant community. A variety of reasons support the extension of the franchise to noncitizens. The reasons range from giving a voice to all individuals in governmental affairs in order to solidify democratic values and the body politic, to the principle that noncitizens have the same obligations as citizens and should therefore enjoy some of the same privileges. However, the main reason to support noncitizen voting is self-preservation. A society's interests are not furthered when a substantial number of its inhabitants are excluded from the body politic and have no meaningful way to petition for a redress of grievances through the electoral process. Such a continued exclusion from political participation is detrimental to achieving a more cohesive society. The ultimate product of such exclusion is a political apartheid.

> *A society's interests are not furthered when a substantial number of its inhabitants . . . have no meaningful way to petition for a redress of grievances through the electoral process.*

The usual avenues for redressing such injustices are judicial actions, legislative proposals, and the initiative process. The prospects of achieving any reform in these ways appear to be highly unlikely, however. In California, a constitutional amendment . . . is necessary to eliminate the United States citizenship requirement for voters. Given the current anti-immigrant climate, any proposed initiative would be doomed to failure. Efforts to declare this citizenship requirement as unconstitutional have been unsuccessful. And any legislative proposals to eliminate the citizenship requirement would be in violation of the state constitution.

Recommendations

Nevertheless, there are several recommendations for pursuing a strategy of noncitizen political empowerment. The world's sixth largest economy simply cannot afford to have a substantial number of persons within its borders who are not politically integrated into the body politic.

1. *Increase Public Debate.* The debate regarding noncitizen disenfranchisement needs to be brought to the forefront, especially given that the noncitizen adult population constitutes a substantial percentage of many communities throughout California. To this end, conferences and symposiums should be convened to formulate strategies for empowering this politically excluded community.

2. Research Current Noncitizen Participation in Local Government. Research should be conducted regarding the eligibility of noncitizens to serve on neighborhood councils and other governmental political subdivisions in California. For example, the 2000 Los Angeles City Charter states that community stakeholders should all have an opportunity to fully participate in the election of Neighborhood Councils Boards. A 2002 City Attorney Opinion reiterated the importance of including all residents irrespective of their citizenship status. The dissemination of these and other examples might eventually create a political climate in which a more comprehensive statewide legislative solution can be effectively pursued. This political climate would be greatly facilitated if the noncitizen population started to flex its economic muscle through the selective use of boycotts, forcing recognition of the significant economic benefits noncitizens contribute and encouraging the political integration of noncitizens through extending the right to vote.

3. Explore Noncitizen Voting for Local Offices. Develop a consensus regarding a constitutional amendment permitting counties, cities, school districts, and other special election districts to determine whether to permit noncitizen voting for local offices. For example, the State of Maryland authorizes municipalities to establish their own voting qualifications, and, as a result, several municipalities permit noncitizens to participate in city elections. Noncitizens can participate in local community board elections in Chicago and New York City. Such an amendment would not affect federal or state offices. And, most significantly, it would not mandate noncitizen voting.

4. Reexamine the Judicial Route. The existence of contrary judicial rulings at the state level should not dissuade legal scholars from investigating alternative legal approaches. For instance, perhaps the right to petition for a redress of grievances incorporates a right to vote. For assistance legal scholars can review the historical transition from the separate but equal doctrine [that legalized discrimination against African Americans] formulated by the United States Supreme Court in *Plessy v. Ferguson* to its abandonment in *Brown v. Board of Education.* Such a transition can serve as a model for the development of legal strategies seeking to remove the citizenship requirement as a qualification for voting. The number of noncitizens revealed by the 2000 U.S. Census may provide a catalyst for the judicial implementation of such a model.

In summary, the exclusion of a growing noncitizen population from the body politic will undermine the participatory electoral process. Rather than maintain a more cohesive society, we will be witnessing the transformation of our cherished democratic institutions into a de facto political apartheid. As a society, we simply cannot afford this outcome.

Organizations to Contact

Black Box Voting
330 SW 43rd St., Suite K, PMB 543, Renton, WA 98055
(206) 335-7747 • (206) 354-5723
e-mail: crew@blackboxvoting.org
Web site: www.blackboxvoting.org

Black Box Voting is a nonpartisan nonprofit consumer protection group for elections, funded by citizen donations. The group's Web site features links to news, forums, and investigations concerning unreliable electronic voting machines, court cases, questionable election outcomes, and other matters concerning voter disenfranchisement due to political machinations.

Cato Institute
1000 Massachusetts Ave. NW, Washington, DC 20001-5403
(202) 842-0200 • fax: (202) 842-3490
e-mail: jblock@cato.org • Web site: www.cato.org

The Cato Institute is a nonprofit libertarian public policy research foundation. The institute seeks to broaden the parameters of public policy debate to allow consideration of the traditional American principles of limited government, individual liberty, free markets and peace. Its publications include *Regulation* magazine; *Cato Policy Report*, a bimonthly newsletter; and *Cato's Letter*, a quarterly newsletter.

Common Cause
1250 Connecticut Ave. NW, Suite 600, Washington, DC 20036
(202) 833-1200
e-mail: grassroots@commoncause.org
Web site: www.commoncause.org

Common Cause is a nonpartisan nonprofit advocacy organization founded in 1970 as a vehicle for citizens to make their voices heard in the political process and to hold their elected leaders accountable to the public interest. With nearly three hundred thousand members Common Cause works to advance campaign reforms, make people and ideas more important than money, remove barriers to voting, and ensure that U.S. voting systems are accurate and accessible. The organization publishes research papers, press releases, e-mail updates, and blogs on its Web site.

Democratic Underground (DU)
PO Box 53350, Washington, DC 20009
e-mail: mail@democraticunderground.com
Web site: www.democraticunderground.com

Democratic Underground was founded on Inauguration Day, January 20, 2001, to protest what it considered the questionable election of George W. Bush as president. The organization provides resources for the exchange and dissemination of liberal and progressive ideas throughout the media. DU publishes original content six days a week and hosts one of the Web's most active left-wing discussion boards.

Election Science Institute
Votewatch Corporation
2269 Chestnut St., Suite 611, San Francisco, CA 94123
fax: (650) 429-2150
Web site: www.votewatch.us

The Election Science Institute (formerly Votewatch) is a nonprofit, nonpartisan and nonadvocacy organization founded to promote transparency in American elections and ensure that every vote cast is counted fairly and accurately. The group's strategy is to bring together county election officials and citizens with expert researchers, engineers, and leading technologies to create model election systems that are auditable and transparent. The group publishes various reports concerning exit polls, voting glitches in local races, and other issues on its Web site.

Fairness and Accuracy in Reporting (FAIR)
112 W. 27th St., New York, NY 10001
(212) 633-6700 • fax: (212) 727-7668
e-mail: fair@fair.org • Web site: www.fair.org

Fairness and Accuracy in Reporting is a national media watchdog group that documents media bias and censorship. FAIR advocates for greater diversity in the press and scrutinizes media practices that marginalize public interest and minority and dissenting viewpoints. FAIR publishes the bimonthly magazine *Extra* that analyzes media treatment of important issues and points out perceived conservative bias.

The Future of Freedom Foundation
11350 Random Hills Rd., Suite 800, Fairfax, Virginia 22030
(703) 934-6101 • fax: (703) 352-8678
e-mail: fff@fff.org • Web site: www.fff.org

The mission of the Future of Freedom Foundation is to advance freedom by providing an uncompromising moral and economic case for individual liberty, free markets, private property, and limited government. The group publishes commentaries, books, e-mail updates, and *Freedom Daily*, a monthly journal of libertarian essays.

Heritage Foundation
214 Massachusetts Ave. NE, Washington, DC 20002
(202) 546-4400 • (800) 544-4843 • fax: (202) 544-2260
e-mail: pubs@heritage.org • Web site: www.heritage.org

The Heritage Foundation is a conservative public policy research institute that supports the principles of free enterprise and limited federal government interference in campaign financing and other election matters. Its many publications include the monthly *Policy Review* and position papers concerning terrorism, election reform, and constitutional issues.

The Hoover Institution
Stanford University, Stanford, CA 94305-6010
(877) 466-8374 • fax: (650) 723-1687
e-mail: horaney@hoover.stanford.edu
Web site: www-hoover.stanford.edu

The Hoover Institution on War, Revolution and Peace, Stanford University, is a conservative public policy research center devoted to advanced study of politics, economics, and political economy—both domestic and foreign—as well as international affairs. Its publications include *Weekly Essays* by Hoover fellows; the *Hoover Digest*, a quarterly journal; and *Policy Review*, a quarterly publication that provides information on matters of public policy.

Public Citizen
215 Pennsylvania Ave. SE, Washington, DC 20003
(202) 546-4996 • fax: (202) 547-7392
e-mail: congress@citizen.org • Web site: www.citizen.org

Public Citizen is a national nonprofit consumer advocacy organization founded in 1971 to represent consumer interests in Congress, the executive branch, and the courts. The Congress Watch division of Public Citizen champions consumer interests before the U.S. Congress and serves as a government watchdog. The group lobbies to demand an end to corporate subsidies to politicians, fights to preserve citizen access to the courts to redress corporate wrongdoing, and seeks to ensure a strong democracy by exposing the harmful impact of money in politics and advocating for comprehensive campaign finance reform. Congress Watch publications include letters to lawmakers, analysis of corporate contributions, and other reports and statements available on the group's Web site.

TomPaine.com
PO Box 53303, Washington, DC 20009
e-mail: editor@tompaine.com • Web site: www.tompaine.com

TomPaine.com is a public interest project of the Institute for America's Future inspired by the eighteenth-century patriot Thomas Paine, author of *Common Sense* and *The Rights of Man*. TomPaine.com seeks to enrich the national debate on controversial public issues by featuring the ideas, opinions, and analyses too often overlooked by the mainstream media. The group's Web site publishes opinion pieces, Web logs, and a page called *News Worthy* that features stories overlooked by the mainstream media.

Verified Voting Foundation
1550 Bryant St., Suite 855, San Francisco, CA 94103
(415) 487-2255 • fax: (928) 244-2347
Web site: www.verifiedvotingfoundation.org

The Verified Voting Foundation is a nonpartisan nonprofit organization championing reliable and publicly verifiable elections. Founded by Stanford University computer science professor David Dill, the organization supports a requirement for voter-verified paper ballots on electronic voting machines, allowing voters to verify individual permanent records of their ballots and election officials to conduct meaningful recounts. The Verified Voting Press Room produces dozens of publications on its Web site under the headings of "Media Releases," "Media Coverage," "Foundation News," and "Foundation Newsletters."

Bibliography

Books

James M. Collier and Kenneth F. Collier — *Votescam: The Stealing of America.* New York: Victoria House, 2000.

Steve Davis — *Click on Democracy: The Internet's Power to Change Political Apathy into Civic Action.* Boulder, CO: Westview, 2002.

Alan M. Dershowitz — *Supreme Injustice: How the High Court Hijacked Election 2000.* New York: Oxford University Press, 2001.

Ronald Dworkin, ed. — *A Badly Flawed Election: Debating* Bush v. Gore, *the Supreme Court, and American Democracy.* New York: New Press, 2002.

John Fund — *Stealing Elections: How Voter Fraud Threatens Our Democracy.* San Francisco: Encounter, 2004.

Jack Germond — *Fat Man Fed Up: How American Politics Went Bad.* New York: Random House, 2004.

Howard Gillman — *The Votes That Counted: How the Court Decided the 2000 Presidential Election.* Chicago: University of Chicago Press, 2001.

Mark Green — *Selling Out: How Big Corporate Money Buys Elections, Rams Through Legislation, and Betrays Our Democracy.* New York: Regan, 2002.

Katherine Harris — *Center of the Storm: Practicing Principled Leadership in Times of Crisis.* Nashville: WND, 2002.

Harry Henderson — *Campaign and Election Reform.* New York: Facts On File, 2004.

Steven Hill — *Fixing Elections: The Failure of America's Winner-Take-All Politics.* New York: Routledge, 2002.

David Horowitz — *How to Beat the Democrats, and Other Subversive Ideas.* Dallas: Spence, 2002.

Martin Merzer — *The* Miami Herald *Report: Democracy Held Hostage.* New York: St. Martin's, 2001.

Anita Miller	*What Went Wrong in Ohio: The Conyers Report on the 2004 Presidential Election.* Chicago: Academy Chicago, 2005.
Mark S. Monmonier	*Bushmanders & Bullwinkles: How Politicians Manipulate Electronic Maps and Census Data to Win Elections.* Chicago: University of Chicago Press, 2001.
Frank Newport	*Polling Matters: Why Leaders Must Listen to the Wisdom of the People.* New York: Warner, 2004.
William Rivers Pitt	*The Greatest Sedition Is Silence: Four Years in America.* Sterling, VA: Pluto, 2003.
Matthew Robinson	*Mobocracy: How the Media's Obsession with Polling Twists the News, Alters Elections, and Undermines Democracy.* Roseville, CA: Forum, 2002.
Bill Sammon	*At Any Cost: How Al Gore Tried to Steal the Election.* Washington, DC: Regnery, 2001.
Steven E. Schier	*You Call This an Election? America's Peculiar Democracy.* Washington, DC: Georgetown University Press, 2003.
Joe Trippi	*The Revolution Will Not Be Televised: Democracy, the Internet, and the Overthrow of Everything.* New York: ReganBooks, 2004.

Periodicals

Sasha Abramsky	"The Redistricting Wars: The Republican Drive Represents a Power Grab Unprecedented in Scale and Timing," *Nation*, December 29, 2003.
J. Kenneth Blackwell	"Technology Matters," *Executive Speeches*, August/September 2002.
Chappell Brown	"Paper Ballots May Be a Better Bet—Electronic Voting Rife with Problems, Says Expert," *Electronic Engineering Times*, November 1, 2004.
Erwin Chemerinsky	"Fairness at the Ballot Box: Several High-Profile Cases Claim That Citizens Who Use Inferior Voting Machines Are Disenfranchised When Others Vote with State-of-the-Art Technology," *Trial*, April 2004.
Marcia Coyle	"Close Vote to Turn on 'Bush v. Gore'?" *National Law Journal*, November 1, 2004.
Clancy DuBos	"A Fight for the Middle: The Motor Voter Law Is Only Part of the Explanation as to Why Voter Turnout Has Dropped Since the Mid-1990s," *Gambit*, October 21, 2003.

Bob Geary	"A Way Out of the Circle of Hell Known as Redistricting," *Independent Weekly*, July 17, 2002.
Jack W. Germond and Jules Witcover	"Polls Haven't Replaced Votes—Yet," *National Journal*, August 14, 1999.
Bev Harris and David Allen	"Can We Trust These Machines?" *Black Box Voting: Ballot Tampering in the 21st Century*. High Point, NC: Plan Nine, 2003.
Steven Hill and Rob Richie	"Voters Lose in Ugly Power Grab," *Colorado Springs Independent*, July 9, 2003.
Anna Kaplan	"Follow the Nonexistent Paper Trail: The Technological Advances in Electronic Voting Machines Raise Accountability Questions About Today's Democratic Process," *Humanist*, January/February 2005.
Alexander Keyssar	"Shoring Up the Right to Vote for President: A Modest Proposal," *Political Science Quarterly*, Summer 2003.
Christine LeVeaux and James C. Garand	"Race-Based Redistricting, Core Constituencies, and Legislative Responsiveness to Constituency Change," *Social Science Quarterly*, March 2003.
Hans S. Nichols	"Redistricting Results Leave GOP Hoping to Make Gains," *Insight on the News*, December 24, 2001.
Eric C. Olson	"Redistricting Reforms," *National Civic Review*, Winter 2002.
Rick Perlstein	"The Case of the Ohio Recount," *Village Voice*, December 22–28, 2004.
Charles Peters	"Safe Seats: Tilting at Windmills," *Washington Monthly*, June 2004.
Debra Rosenberg	"A Long Shadow; *Bush v. Gore* Roiled a Nation. It's Back—and, Given Rehnquist's Health, Looming Larger than Ever," *Newsweek*, November 8, 2004.
Tara Ross	"The Electoral College Wins Again," *American Enterprise*, January/February 2005.
Lester Kenyatta Spence, James L. Gibson, and Gregory A. Caldeira	"The Supreme Court and the US Presidential Election of 2000: Wounds, Self-Inflicted or Otherwise?" *British Journal of Political Science*, October 2003.
Jeffrey Toobin	"The Great Election Grab: U.S. Supreme Court to Consider Complex Question of Redistricting and Its Potential Abuse," *New Yorker*, December 8, 2003.

Laurence Tribe
"The Unbearable Wrongness of *Bush v. Gore*," *Constitutional Commentary*, Winter 2002.

Dan Verton and
Patrick Thibodeau
"Electronic Voting Systems Pass Their Big Test—Maybe: Vendors Say Election Validates Technology; Critics Not Convinced," *Computerworld*, November 8, 2004.

David I. Wells
"Degrees of Democracy: Rethinking the Electoral College," *New Leader*, November/December 2004.

Bob Wing
"The White Elephant in the Room: Race and Election 2004," *Independent Politics News*, Winter 2005.

Index

Abdi, Nuradin, 72
absentee ballots, 10
AccuVote machines, 53
African Americans,
  disempowered from voting,
  61–63, 68
Alabama election (2002),
  41–42
Allamakee County, Iowa
  election (2000), 45–46
Allen, David, 41
Amar, Akhil Reed, 11
Andrew, Joe, 53–54
Arian, Sami Al-, 72
Askew, Reubin, 18–19
Association of Community
  Organization for Reform
  Now (ACORN), 72
Avila, Joaquin, 74

Baehr, Richard A., 11
Bernalillo County, New
  Mexico, 50
Bipartisan Campaign Reform
  Act. See McCain-Feingold
  bill
Bradley, Bill, 17
Britain, Williams J., 57
Brown, Sherrod, 17
Bryan, William Jennings, 25
Buhler, Roman, 58
butterfly ballots, 10
Byrd, Robert C., 17–18

campaign finance reform
  corporations and, 25, 26–27
  historical background to,
  25–26

incumbency and, 16–17
lack of confidence in
  democracy and, 24–25
in McCain-Feingold bill,
  22–23
misuse of government
  power with, 23–24
Caracas (Venezuela), 48
Chavez, Hugo, 48
Clay County, Kansas, 43
Cleland, Max, 53
Corzine, Jon, 20
Cotter, Joe, 49
Cramer, Howard, 50

Dade County, Florida, 49
Dallas, Texas, 47–48
Dayton, Mark, 20
democracy
  campaign finance reform
  and, 24–25
  electoral-vote system and,
  30–31, 34, 40
Democrats, 20, 23, 54–55, 73
Diebold (company), 49, 52,
  53, 56–57
direct-recording electronic
  machines (DREs). See
  electronic voting machines
Dole, Elizabeth, 18
Durbin, Dick, 17

Edwards, George C., III,
  30–31, 35
Electoral Systems Software
  (ES&S), 41–42, 46, 47–48
electoral-vote system
  advantages of two-party

system and, 38–39
direct election vs., 39–40
the disenfranchised and,
   28–29
effects of dismantling,
   33–34, 36–37
election of 2000 exposing
   problems in, 9–11
Framers' intent with, 37–38
ignores diversity of public
   opinions, 32–33
is an antidemocratic
   procedure, 29–31
con, 40
overrepresents small states,
   31–32
public opinion on, 34–35,
   37
electronic voting machines
conspiracy theories about,
   51–55
incorrect programming of,
   48–50
miscounted votes/glitches
   with, 41–48
security of, 55–58
Eschberger, Tom, 47
Espinoza, Arthur, 43

Faris, Iyman, 72
Faulkner, Bob, 45
Federal Election Commission
   (FEC), 23
Federation for American
   Immigration Reform (FAIR),
   72–73
Feingold, Russell, 22
felons
prohibited from voting,
   59–65
restoring voting rights for,
   65–67
Filkins, Dexter, 19
Fitzgerald, Peter, 20

527 committees, 23
Florida, 9–11
France, Anatole, 19
France, voter turnout in, 13,
   14
Frost, Martin, 16
Fund, John, 51, 72

Gans, Curtis, 14
Garofolo, Lisa, 46
Gentry, Michael, 10
Georgia election (2002), 53
Glass, Carter, 62
Global Election Management
   System, 49, 53
Great Compromise, the, 31
Green, Mark, 13

Hagel, Chuck, 45
Hanna, Mark, 25
Harris, Bev, 41, 52–53, 56
Hastert, Dennis, 16
Helander, Willard, 49
Holt, Rush, 58
*House Insurance: How the
   Permanent Congress Hoards
   Campaign Cash* (study), 16
House of Representatives,
   U.S., 31
Hull, Elizabeth, 59
Human Rights Watch, 61

illegal aliens. *See* noncitizens,
   voting by

Jefferson, Thomas, 37–38
Jones, Daryl, 63

Kane County, Illinois, 43
Kelley, Mark, 42
Kerry, John, 20
King, Steve, 58
Kohl, Herbert, 20
Kousser, Morgan, 62

Lake County, Illinois, 49
Lapham, Lewis H., 28
Las Vegas, Nevada, 43
Leadership Conference on
  Civil Rights, 54
League of Women Voters, 62
Le Pen, Jean-Marie, 14
Levin, Carl, 20
Lewis, Linda, 46
Lytel, Elaine, 45

Malkin, Michelle, 71
McCain, John, 22
McCain-Feingold bill, 23, 24,
  40
McKinley, William, 25–26
McLennan County, Texas, 46
McMillan, Malcolm, 62
Media Fund, 23
MicroVote machines, 46
Miholic, Richard, 42–43

National Commission on
  Federal Election Reform, 66
Nebraska, 14
Nixon, Richard M., 39
noncitizens, voting by
  citizenship status of election
    workers and, 72–73
  Latino political
    empowerment and, 74–75
  reasons for, 75–76
  recommendations for
    pursuing, 76–78
  terrorist suspects and, 71–72

O'Dell, Walden, 52, 56
Ohio, 72
Oklahoma election (1997),
  44
Onondaga County, New
  York, 45
optical scan voting system,
  55, 57

Peevy, Donn, 44
Pima County, Arizona, 48–49
political fundraising, 14–21
  see also campaign finance
    reform
presidential election(s), 14,
  25–26, 38–39
  2000, 9–11, 30, 32–33, 49,
    51–52
  2004, 28–29, 34
Public Citizen's Congress
  Watch, 16
public opinion, 11, 34–35, 37
punch-card voting system, 55

al Qaeda members, voting by,
  71–72

Republicans, 23
Richman, Sheldon, 22
Riley, Bob, 42
Rivera, Rafael, 49
Rockefeller, Jay, 20
Romero, Richard, 50
Roosevelt, Theodore, 25
Rosenfeld, Richard, 31
Rosenkranz, Joshua, 18

Schmitt, Mark, 21
Scurry County, Texas, 43–44
Senate, U.S., 31
Sentencing Project, The, 61
Shamos, Michael, 55–56
Sheinbaum, Stanley, 18
Siegelman, Don, 42
Sitkoff, Robert H., 25, 26
Smith, Hal, 43
Standard Oil, 26
Supreme Court, U.S., 11, 20,
  60

Taylor, M.A., 47
Tillman Act (1907), 25, 26
Tomatsu, Deloitte Touche, 27

Tozzo, Christopher M., 68
Tucson, Arizona, 47

Uhlmann, Michael M., 36
United Kingdom, voter
  turnout in, 13
Urosevich, Bob, 45

vote recounts, 9–10
voter participation, 13–15
voting machines. *See*

electronic voting machines

Wallace, George, 39
West, Kevin, 47
Weyrich, Paul, 15
Wilson, James Q., 64
Wisconsin, 72–73
Wright, J. Skelly, 19
Wyden, Ron, 17

Zevin, Susan, 56